**Towards the goal of full employment**

# Towards the goal of full employment

## Trends, obstacles and policies

**Peter Richards**

INTERNATIONAL LABOUR OFFICE • GENEVA

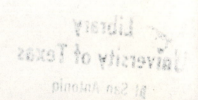

Richards, P.
*Towards the goal of full employment: Trends, obstacles and policies*
Geneva, International Labour Office, 2001
Full employment, promotion of employment, employment policy, developed country, developing country. 13.03.3

ISBN 92-2-111389-2

*ILO Cataloguing in Publication Data*

Printed and bound in the United Kingdom by Biddles Ltd, *www.biddles.co.uk*

# CONTENTS

**List of tables**

**List of figures**

# ABBREVIATIONS AND ACRONYMS

| | |
|---|---|
| AIDS | Acquired Immune Deficiency Syndrome |
| CEPR | country employment policy review |
| CIS | Commonwealth of Independent States |
| Comecon | Council for Mutual Economic Assistance |
| ECE | Economic Commission for Europe |
| EPL | employment protection legislation |
| EPZ | export processing zone |
| EU | European Union |
| EU-15 | 15 Member States of the European Union |
| GDP | gross domestic product |
| HIV | human immunodeficiency virus |
| ICRG | international country risk guide |
| IFI | international financial institution |
| ILO | International Labour Office/Organization |
| IMF | International Monetary Fund |
| IPF | investment and privatization fund |
| IS | import substitution |
| IT | information technology |
| KILM | Key Indicators of the Labour Market (ILO publication) |
| NAFTA | North American Free Trade Agreement |
| NMP | net material product |
| OECD | Organisation for Economic Co-operation and Development |
| SPA | State Property Agency |
| TFP | total factor productivity |
| TVE | township and village enterprise |

# ACKNOWLEDGEMENTS

The author would like to thank the following colleagues for their ideas or short drafts that are reflected or appear in certain sections of the text: Ajit Ghose (Chapter 2, part 2.2 – *Asia*), Steven Oates (Chapter 2, part 2.3 – *Freedom of association*), and Janine Rodgers and Constance Thomas (Chapter 2, part 2.3 – *The promotion of women in the labour force, discrimination and equality of opportunity*).

# PREFACE

This study takes as its point of departure a report presented to an International Labour Organization (ILO) meeting in November 1999,[1] which was intended to stimulate discussion within the ILO's tripartite constituency on the contribution that the ILO could make to the World Summit for Social Development and the United Nations Special Session on Follow-up to the World Summit for Social Development (Copenhagen, 1995, and Geneva, 2000, respectively). The 1999 report documents the ILO's view of how best to help solve the world's employment problems, drawing on ILO instruments (that is, Conventions and Recommendations), conclusions of its General Conference and other similar consensual statements, with the help of a number of regional papers prepared by external experts. This study acknowledges these external contributions where they have been extensively drawn on as well as the contributions of colleagues from the ILO. Only for the sake of convenience does this study have a single named author, who is the first to accept that he is, more accurately speaking, the compiler of, and a contributor to, this report.

*Towards the goal of full employment: Trends, obstacles and policies* takes the 1999 report further. It documents the current world employment situation, how the latter falls short of what it could be, how current economic policies of market liberalization are interacting with the world employment situation and how the employment situation could be improved. Meeting the commitment that so many governments have made to achieving full employment is, in large part, a matter of national policies, reflecting national circumstances and the operation of institutions developed to reflect national concerns. Nonetheless, it is equally important to emphasize that there are a number of general rules and aspirations that are applicable everywhere and which can form the basis of a common employment strategy. In addition, since so many countries have adopted broadly similar economic policies, many of the employment problems they face have similar characteristics and call for the same kind of corrective action. ILO guidelines, in the form of standards and Recommendations, give a great deal of help in this respect.

The aim of this study is to present the world employment situation in as realistic a way as possible and to show that, as a certainly complex issue, it is not simply an aggregation of numbers of people at work or seeking work; issues of employment quality, such as freedom of association and participation, discrimination and equal opportunity, are given considerable attention. It is stressed that labour market behaviour and workers' approaches to employment vary significantly between countries, partly because of different regulatory regimes (such as those of the more industrialized economies), but more importantly because of overall income differences between countries at different stages of development. The study also demonstrates that labour market behaviour and employment quality do interact with the economic policy framework that is being followed. However, the study is at pains to stress that describing the evolution of employment in a country is not the same as describing how that economy evolved, and that even additionally undertaking an analysis of the behaviour of national income distribution at the household level does not equate to an analysis of employment developments. Therefore, the idea is to help readers come to understand employment as something that is highly dependent on national circumstances and institutions, and distinct from just incomes and economic growth.

Another aim of this study is to demonstrate how the ILO contributes to helping improve the world employment situation, which it does both by encouraging a comprehensive approach to viewing employment issues and by giving advice on specific policy areas. The ILO's comprehensive and partly standard-setting approach to employment issues effectively sets the parameters for a national employment strategy.

Chapter 1 sets the scene by reviewing the implications for national action of the ILO's Employment Policy Convention, 1964 (No. 122), and the various attributes of employment and unemployment that apply nationally and worldwide. It also discusses some of the levers that make up an employment strategy, which can be used to move the employment situation closer to a position of full employment. Chapter 2 looks at the world employment situation – overall and by region – as well as at developments in some aspects of employment quality, including freedom of association and equal opportunity. Chapter 3 examines some recent policy experience, contrasting East and South-East Asia with Latin America and studying the developments in the 1990s in most of the Organisation for Economic

Cooperation and Development (OECD) member countries and in Central and Eastern Europe. Chapter 4 concludes by looking, firstly, at some aspects of poverty and income distribution, then at the criticisms directed at existing policies and, finally, at the ILO's contribution to ensuring socially acceptable outcomes of the growth process.

## Note

[1] "The International Labour Organization and the promotion of full, productive and freely chosen employment", presented to the International Consultation concerning Follow-up to the World Summit for Social Development, Nov. 1999.

# THE COMMITMENT TO FULL EMPLOYMENT

# 1

## 1.1 introduction

In the summer of 1964 the ILO added to its already extensive battery of labour standards (which serve as guidelines to national legislation in the labour field) the Employment Policy Convention (No. 122), committing future ratifying States to "declare and pursue as a major goal an active policy designed to promote full, productive and freely chosen employment".[1] In the past decade, renewed emphasis on an official commitment to achieving full employment was given by the World Summit for Social Development, held in Copenhagen in 1995, and the follow-up 24th Special Session of the General Assembly of the United Nations in Geneva, 2000. The commitment to achieving full employment with full respect for workers' rights made at the World Summit for Social Development owes much to the ILO's earlier Conventions.

Countries that have ratified the ILO Employment Policy Convention, 1964 (No. 122), are obliged to report on the action they have taken to bring about full employment.[2] This obligation has, however, raised two interrelated sets of issues. The first is the problem of recognizing the state of full, productive and freely chosen employment once it has been reached. At no time has the ILO offered any explanation as to what constitutes full employment, particularly in a developing country context, in order to measure any shortfall. Nor has any explicit test been proposed for ascertaining full employment in industrialized countries. The reason for the latter seems to be that during the early 1960s open unemployment in OECD member countries and in Central and Eastern Europe was extremely low. What constituted full employment (over and above "frictional" unemployment levels of 2–3 per cent) seemed obvious. The fact that in the former set of countries female labour force participation rates were also very low was not seen as relevant to a definition of full employment (see Section 1.2 of this chapter for a discussion on the definition and measurement of employment and unemployment).

The second issue raised is the problem of identifying an economic and social (employment) strategy that will achieve the desirable state of full employment. (Some basic elements of an employment strategy are discussed in Section 1.3, both in a general context and for developing, industrialized and transition countries separately.) An employment strategy will have similarities with an economic strategy delivering broad-based and poverty-alleviating growth. But the notion of achieving full and productive employment goes beyond that of attaining sustained growth in output by incorporating both distributional and participatory elements. Furthermore, growth is not always necessary to sustain full employment. However, growth is generally a prerequisite for overcoming unemployment and raising the quality of jobs and, to that extent, the two goals operate in parallel. In addition, full employment in a well-functioning market economy should itself be a guarantee of growth (see below).

Some observers feel that they have now found the key to obtaining full employment; in the European Union (EU), for example, there is much optimism that the steps necessary to achieve it have been found.[3] This optimism stems partly from the fact that the focus of the EU's employment policies is principally on reducing unemployment through active labour market policies, although there are few links between EU countries' labour market and macroeconomic policies (see Chapter 3), and partly because EU countries suffer few of the constraints experienced by much of the developing world. Even within the EU different regulatory approaches to labour market functioning are felt to be consistent with achieving similar outcomes in different societies, and actual outcomes in terms of employment growth have, indeed, varied greatly across the Union. The relative importance of issues such as fewer working hours or greater or lesser levels of labour force participation also varies within the EU. Thus, there is within the EU a lack of complete agreement both on what full employment should be and on how exactly it should be achieved. Nonetheless, many of the methods being used by the EU to overcome unemployment through active labour market measures would form part of an ideal employment strategy.

More broadly, there is now considerable support worldwide for a neo-liberal approach to economic policy, which many feel will produce both output growth and good employment results by raising the demand for labour (and possibly also by increasing competition in the labour market).[4]

There are, however, certain preconditions to the success of this model: it cannot work effectively unless markets are fully competitive; governments operate wisely; and there is full equality of opportunity. Chapters 3 and 4 discuss whether and under which conditions this policy of market liberalization can secure desirable employment goals.

A recent formulation of the ILO's role in aiding its constituents has been to "promote opportunities for women and men to obtain decent and productive work".[5] The aim of the so-called "decent work" programme is to secure full employment together with universal respect for fundamental principles and rights at work (ILO Declaration on Fundamental Principles and Rights at Work and its Follow-up, 1998), including social dialogue (freedom of association and collective bargaining), the absence of discrimination, of forced labour and especially of the worst forms of child labour, and social protection. To a large extent, the achievement of full, productive and freely chosen employment involves respect for rights at work, non-discrimination in hiring and in opportunities for acquiring skills and, by definition, the absence of forced labour. These are all elements of what is described later in this chapter as good or high-quality employment. Indeed, they all proceed from a set of values that both cherishes individual freedoms and opportunities and respects the desire of workers and employers to pursue common and legitimate objectives with like-minded individuals.

But although widely accepted officially, this set of values easily comes into conflict with other social norms regarding gender hierarchy, kinship and ethnic group relations. Nearly all societies practise some form of discrimination, which they justify in terms of the high social or business costs that implementing non-discrimination rules would incur. Many societies also place restrictions on freedom of association, partly because governments often take sides in alleged social class conflicts, partly because of fears that legitimate forms of protest will be used irresponsibly. For all these reasons, a decent work strategy is rarely fully respected, although there is probably common agreement that some lapses are more serious than others. Yet, there are strong arguments that progress towards meeting the Decent Work Agenda will contribute to ensuring that the process of growth is equitable and socially acceptable. This, in turn, can lead to both better policy-making and more willing burden-sharing in times of difficulty.

The concept of social protection, which is also contained within a decent work strategy, is complex. Decent work encompasses a certain degree of income and job security. However, countries differ greatly in the extent to which they expect individual workers to respond to unforeseen (job loss) and foreseeable (old age) falls in income. In terms of the costs and benefits of providing greater income and job security, the benefits (harmony at the workplace, a greater willingness on the part of workers and employers to seek and provide training) but also a fear of the costs are generally acknowledged. These costs can range from labour market rigidity (excessive job security) to moral hazard (high non-work benefits) to perverse effects on income distribution (topping up skilled workers' savings from general tax revenues). There is, therefore, quite considerable scope for debate on the appropriate levels of, and the design of institutions for, job and income security.

Decent work also provides a focus for issues of poverty and income inequality, both nationally and globally. Firstly, decent work means little as a concept if workers are not ensured an "adequate" income. This should preclude the need to "overwork" and allow for sufficient rest and time for family responsibilities. It should also eliminate the need for sustained child labour to add to the family income, or to free up parents' time by the children taking on excessive domestic responsibilities. Continued poverty is an antithesis of decent work. In addition, if within the same country you have continued poverty on the one hand and a vibrant demand for more highly educated workers on the other, this will inevitably lead to a worsening distribution of income. This might suggest that effective discrimination exists between different parts of the labour force, thereby restricting occupational mobility. Therefore, a worsening income distribution may be reflecting the interplay of market forces but be set against a particular institutional background, which could be altered by giving greater assistance to the education and training of the poor. In a similar vein, and perhaps in wealthier countries, a widening distribution of earnings could reflect a weakening of workers' ability to bargain collectively, which could be the outcome of government efforts to achieve labour market flexibility, by means which are incompatible with a system of consensual negotiation and agreement. A worsening inter-country distribution of income could also represent the continued presence of poverty concentrated in a few countries or regions. All this suggests that, without taking an explicit stance on what should be the extent of a desirable distribution of income, a decent work strategy should direct attention at the issues of poverty alleviation, discrimination in access to jobs (and, very possibly, in access to the preconditions for obtaining jobs) and the bargaining power of the workforce.

## 1.2   Measuring and defining employment and unemployment

What does or did the ILO expect a situation of full employment to resemble? Some idea of this and related issues of measurement would seem to be necessary if progress towards achieving full employment is to be assessed. A prerequisite must be a low recorded rate of unemployment; anything else would not be credible. Whether the unemployment data used should be those generated by administrative sources, that is, usually those people registered for drawing benefit, or by labour force surveys was not initially addressed as an issue. Only in 1982 did the Thirteenth International Conference of Labour Statisticians agree that labour force surveys were to be the preferred source of data collection, although the use of other means of data was not to be precluded.[6] The ILO did set internationally compatible guidelines for the measurement of employment and unemployment through labour force surveys. The first guidelines resulted from the Eighth International Conference of Labour Statisticians in 1954. But seeds of confusion were, nevertheless, sown, since the criteria for being counted as unemployed were strict; for example, working (for pay or profit, or as an unpaid family worker) for just one hour in the reference week was sufficient for an individual to count as employed. (The guidelines always referred to "some work" in the reference week.) Furthermore, employment status always has priority over other forms of activity; if, for example, someone is both studying and working, that person is reported as employed. The result of the phrasing of the guidelines was threefold: firstly, some countries showed an extremely and, at first sight, improbably low rate of unemployment, largely because few individuals could afford to be without any work (India is a prime example); secondly, many of those people reported as unemployed were holding out for more attractive jobs (a part, at least, of the phenomenon of "educated unemployed");[7] and, thirdly, other indicators began to be collected which it was felt gave a truer picture of supply and demand in the labour market, particularly in poorer countries.[8]

These supplementary indicators included measures of under-employment, such as involuntary part-time work (that is, those people wanting to work more hours than a stated number), working for very low incomes and working at a task where acquired education and skills are not needed. Calculating the employed as a share of the population of working age and not of the labour force is another means of measuring underemployment.[9] But while using a range of indicators is necessary to describe the labour market situation in one country, inter-country comparisons will, inevitably, demand a simpler approach, even if this may, in many ways, be misleading. Furthermore, many of the indicators only raise further questions. Working long hours for little money is surely as much a labour market failure as involuntary part-time work and, in the last resort, what is special about the labour market "success" that, perhaps by weakening the incomes of the unskilled, pulls more and more people into jobs? How voluntary are decisions taken in the wake of a breakdown in, for example, family support and sharing systems, or perhaps of a collapse in unemployment benefit systems, which severely limits the possibilities for job search?

A consequence of the difficulties inherent in choosing and using indicators is that different regions of the world adopt different forms of measurement or measure different things. Thus, in Latin America, for example, two features have emerged. Firstly, and perhaps surprisingly, open unemployment rates have been given more "content" by being shown to be often directly correlated with household poverty, even using adult equivalence scales to avoid the phenomenon of households with more children automatically being counted as poorer. Although unemployment data are collected for urban areas only, unemployment levels have shown an upward trend in recent years, irrespective of cyclical features. As A. Berry and M. T. Mendez have remarked,[10] the trade-off between output growth and employment, which has usually been observed in Latin America, remains, although its nature has changed. However, the indicator usually associated with this region is the size of the urban informal sector, which has been taken as an indicator of welfare (because informal sector workers are in a relatively weak labour market position) as well as a cyclical indicator. It is now losing its value in the second respect, since it no longer seems to respond to cyclical upswings (largely because larger enterprises no longer seem to be creating any new jobs), and may also be losing its information value in the first respect. The definitional limits of the urban informal sector are themselves fairly informal, but the concept has been found to be useful within the regional context.[11]

In OECD member countries and, above all, in Western Europe, some analysts have become disillusioned with the use of the unemployment rate as an indicator, largely because governments have deprived the indicator of much of its content. This has been done by instituting programmes in which some workers have been removed from the labour force altogether (through, for example, introducing a lower retirement age and inappropriate definitions of disability) or by "occupying" some of the unemployed in training and other "transitional" schemes, during the course of which they are counted as "employed". Many potential workers have thus become "unavailable" for ordinary work in a statistical sense, even though they may consider themselves as unemployed. Consequently, emphasis has been laid on measuring the share of the population of working age that is employed, so that what is left is the "non-employment rate", whether this consists of those genuinely seeking work or not. A logical extension of this approach would be to have a target employment to population rate, since there is no longer agreement on the nature of the unemployment rate that is to be minimized, so no other guide to policy. But, as any comparison of Western European countries will show, the employment to population rate varies so much (just as many social practices vary, in particular, the role of the household in childcare) that it makes little sense to aim at maximizing it.[12] As a result, employment policy in Western Europe is not concerned with ends and targets (except for retraining programmes) but with environments and frameworks.

In Eastern Europe the situation is very different. Paradoxically, before the fall of communism the area was more concerned with the overall labour supply and with having as many workers employed as possible than with measuring unemployment levels. This has now changed, and because, for example, assisted early retirement is less common than in Western Europe, unemployment rates, at least in Central Europe, are fairly reliable indicators of labour market behaviour. Most Central European countries collect both labour force survey and administrative data on unemployment. Survey data generally show lower unemployment levels than unemployment registers. However, where labour hoarding within the enterprise is common, such as in parts of the Commonwealth of Independent States (CIS), in China and Viet Nam, unemployment rate data have little informational value. And in places such as China, where rural-urban migration is severely restricted, the urban unemployment rate is a poor indicator of national labour market trends; rural-based jobseekers are simply not included in the unemployment figures.

The approach to labour market indicators in Asia has partly gone in the direction of measuring wage and non-wage incomes. D. Mazumdar[13] has described how the concept of "turning points", taken from Arthur Lewis,[14] has been used to track the period when the virtual stagnation of the wages of rural, unskilled workers began to give way to a rise more or less in line with overall per capita income. Even if finding that precise moment has usually proved elusive, the approach has focused attention on the issue of rural-urban interaction in economies with free migration, unlike the usual focus on urban areas only in, for example, Latin America. Certainly in Indonesia, Mazumdar has shown that it is possible to single out a period where sustained wage growth did begin (circa 1990–95), and similar claims have been made in relation to Japan, the Republic of Korea and Taiwan (China). And the attention paid to following the behaviour of the

7

(real) wages of unskilled workers has helped provide a yardstick for measuring the success of many forms of government intervention aimed at raising welfare and reducing poverty in general.

When in a recent article,[15] A. K. Sen diagnosed the nature of employment, he made a distinction between a production aspect and an income aspect. This distinction was necessary because any activity can be subsidized to yield an income, even if to observers the activity is apparently unproductive. Sen also described the position of the family farm with surplus labour, a situation that, even without family ownership, can be mirrored in some state-owned enterprises, where workers can be unemployed from one point of view (that is, they can be surplus to calculated requirements) but still draw an income.[16]

Sen also diagnosed a third aspect of employment: that of recognition. He saw this as taking two forms: self-recognition and societal recognition. Self-recognition concerns undertaking work that one does not recognize as adequate and appropriate, so that one can therefore be "unemployed" in the sense that one is available for what is considered more suitable work. Societal recognition applies to the refusal of society to consider that, for example, household work has an economic as well as a domestic value. The recognition aspect can be given a further dimension, concerning not only a recognition of the value of the activity being carried out but also of the rights and duties inherent in the employment relationship and its means of negotiation. In this case, recognition comes from society at large and usually in the form of legislation.

In addressing the 87th Session of the International Labour Conference, 1999, and commenting on the Director-General's report, *Decent work* (see endnote 5), Sen took the concept of rights even further. He stressed that people have, for example, the right to a life without hunger, even if no particular person or agency has a corresponding obligation to fulfil that right. Such rights are claims addressed to anyone who can help, and recognizing them as rights should make their fulfilment more probable.

The ILO's Employment Policy Convention, 1964 (No. 122), states not only that employment should be "full", hence the measurement issues being discussed here, but that individual jobs should be productive and freely chosen. The concept of a productive job is partly that it should be recognized as such, that is, that there needs to be common acceptance that a job is in some way adding value to the community and involves producing something that others also value. In this sense one's own domestic work is not a job, because it is only of value to oneself and to one's immediate family. But no definition is ever watertight. If, for example, to paraphrase a common example used in national income accounting, a businesswoman marries her chauffeur, who continues to drive her to work, has his task become unproductive?

"Freely chosen" was no doubt intended to exclude the practice of the direction of labour[17] and forced labour[18] and should perhaps be seen more in terms of an established right to leave a job than of having a choice between roughly similar jobs. However, someone can freely choose a particular job where the right to leave is restricted and far from cost-free. "Freely chosen" also has an echo of Sen's recognition effect in that a job which is not freely chosen is unlikely to be personally recognized as appropriate, although in some circumstances society might call the job necessary and productive.

Differences in measuring the characteristics of employment across regions, which lead to restrictions on accurately describing a global employment picture, are partly, but not entirely, the consequence of different economic structures in countries at various income levels and a resulting larger or smaller number of wage or self-employed workers. Wage workers, but not the self-employed,[19] are in an employment relationship, although this relationship gives little protection against economic fluctuations and risks of income loss. (This is not to rule out workers' acceptance of a low but steady wage, while owners are exposed to the risk of intermittent losses.) Where such explicit income protection is given, it is generally done through the State by unemployment benefits. This, of course, is a major and well-recorded distinction between richer and poorer countries that has considerable implications for labour market functioning and that makes a comparison between the labour market and employment statistics of such countries extremely difficult to draw.

This action by the State is not the only reason why it is so difficult to make comparisons of different employment situations between countries at very different relative income levels. The issue of excessive work or overwork also needs to be discussed. Overwork can be defined as occurring when the value of leisure time is relegated to almost zero, with no time left for a full night's sleep. In the worst-case scenario, this occurs when the contribution to income of an additional unit of work is declining but total income is nonetheless below a necessary or desired level. This is the condition which Mazumdar describes as prevailing in many agricultural households in poor countries. Off season, family members are involved in a number of low-productivity activities, yielding less per day than their main agricultural work. Thus they are not recorded by labour force surveys as being "involuntarily unemployed". There are vestiges of this problem in wealthier countries; one response to falling real wages for unskilled workers over a long period in the United States was for families to work longer hours, often drawing on previously inactive family members, whose average wage was even lower than that of existing workers.[20] Child labour is part of this phenomenon, but is usually more often a consequence of absolute rather than relative poverty. However, seeking additional work, even on the poor terms of declining income per unit of time, is no guarantee that such work will be found. And whether additional work is found or not, the situation is obviously unsatisfactory.

This brings us back to the issue of the growth of incomes and output. As discussed in Chapter 4, the alleviation of poverty almost by definition requires an increase in incomes per capita and thus overall growth. To overcome labour underutilization, there has to be an increase in the demand for labour, which is derived from faster output growth. The absence of growth perpetuates underemployment and poverty where they already exist. Logically, a sufficiently wealthy country with full employment may not need faster growth and can instead increase leisure time. Equally logically, a sufficiently wealthy country with a degree of unemployment can share out income-earning opportunities and forego employment growth at existing levels of productivity. In fact, largely for microeconomic reasons, neither of the last two propositions is likely to hold. A wealthy country with a well-educated workforce will absorb new technology and grow as fast as its peers. Deliberate work-sharing will not generate new jobs if productivity increases, as it may well, and increasing the number of low-productivity jobs in order to absorb the unemployed needs growth and may also create additional problems (see Chapter 3). Growth, meanwhile, greatly eases the resource mobilizing role of government. In general, therefore, growth is important for full employment in all countries, just as its distributional impact is important for alleviating poverty.[21]

It is useful to recall that when the ILO's World Employment Programme began in the late 1960s, there were many calls to "dethrone GDP". Essentially, this meant giving social and economic objectives equal weight in national policy formulation, and usually it was felt that this could only work if radical changes were made in asset ownership. Commenting on his proposed programme for Colombia, Dudley Seers, the then director of the Institute of Development Studies at the University of Sussex (United Kingdom), suggested that, so far as the poor were concerned, faster growth meant greater inequality and thus constant and continued poverty.[22] Today, this stance would be regarded as extreme. On the other hand, the early ILO comprehensive employment strategy missions led by Dudley Seers (to Colombia and Sri Lanka) in the early 1970s demonstrated that meeting the objectives of full employment would necessarily generate faster growth. This realization did not make the obstacles to growth in developing countries, such as lack of skills, capital and foreign exchange, any less real or binding. However, it did suggest that better policies would lead to a better use of the workforce, which is what sustained and job-creating growth is all about. Furthermore, it dispelled the pessimistic notion that employment-oriented development might slow down growth, an idea entertained by the ILO's then Director-General, David Morse, in 1968.[23]

Around the world workers with an employment relationship clearly have common interests, and many of the ILO's activities have been directed at clarifying and improving such employment relationships – to the extent that some observers have questioned whether the ILO is concerned with *all* workers. The situation of employed workers can be compared in terms of, for example, length of tenure, skills acquisition, conditions of work and freedom of association. Of course, in many countries such features can only be realistically discussed with a minority of workers in mind. This again makes presenting a view of the world employment situation difficult, and thus indicates that a region-by-region approach, where circumstances are likely to be more uniform, would be more suitable.

The ILO's notion of what is a desirable state of employment has a number of other aspects – as has been brought out in the discussion of decent work. Firstly, there must be freedom for workers and employers to associate and form federations at national (and international) level. Secondly, there should be no discrimination. Within the fields of competence of the ILO, discrimination is defined as any distinction, whether exclusion or preference, based on race, colour, sex, religion, political opinion, national extraction or social origin (or any other ground so designated at the national level) that nullifies or impairs equality of opportunity or treatment in employment or occupation. This definition covers access to training, employment, occupation as well as terms and conditions of employment. Protection should also be given against discrimination based on trade union membership, nationality, disability, family responsibilities, pregnancy and age. Other, more recent, grounds include state of health – to protect, for example, people with acquired immune deficiency syndrome (AIDS) or human immunodeficiency virus (HIV) – and sexual orientation.[24]

So far as freedom of association is concerned, the conditions under which groups of wage earners, self-employed agricultural workers or artisans, or, indeed, employers can join forces to further and defend their collective interests have an enormous bearing on welfare at work. Both de jure and de facto, freedom of association enables workers to negotiate their working and living conditions as a collective body and to define, for themselves, what is acceptable. Theoretically at least, such organizations ensure that all workers have a say in their working life. When grouped together in federations or confederations at a higher and broader level, these organizations can be a powerful instrument for changing basic aspects and beliefs of civil society. Actively discouraging the formation of such organizations and their amalgamation into higher-level federations, putting constraints on their operation, or robbing them of independence by assimilating them into a totalitarian power structure are all means of reducing the quality of work.

Other aspects of good employment quality include respect for health and safety measures, the provision of some employment and income security, individual fulfilment at work and equality of opportunity or the absence of discrimination. In general, these aspects of employment quality cannot be perfectly quantified. To some extent, either income or some measure of civil liberties can stand as a proxy for them.[25] This, in turn, suggests that some are absolute (such as freedom of association) and some contingent on the level of economic development. Or, in terms of rights, some are more easily fulfilled (that is, through legislation rather than through decades of development) than others.

In short, the state of "full, productive and freely chosen employment" can be said to exist where there is neither overwork nor insufficient work, no absolute poverty and no discrimination. Those workers who enjoy an employment relationship should be able to exercise the rights that the State guarantees and be satisfied that their work is productive. Independent workers should also be confident of enjoying some basic rights and freedoms, such as support in old age. And what kind of employment policy is likely to get closest to this ideal? To try and help answer this question, the next section reviews the context in which employment policies directed at achieving this ideal operate.

## 1.3 An employment strategy: Common elements and variations

Is there a common, universal set of rules, principles and procedures for an employment strategy that could be applied to every single country? The aim of an employment strategy is to raise the quality of jobs for all, preferably beginning with those workers whose job quality is least satisfactory. As to whom belongs to this group, this would be a matter to be settled nationally by consensus. Broad statistical categories of occupations, however, give some pointers (see the discussion at the beginning of Chapter 2). Two questions that immediately arise concern, firstly, the status of the unemployed: are the unemployed, under all circumstances, those members of the labour force section most in need of help[26] and what is the status of discouraged workers? And is aiming for a high labour force participation rate, as is frequently suggested by the European Commission, a desirable aim? Answers to both questions are likely to be country specific.

A procedural approach to formulating an employment strategy would generally begin by assessing whether past growth has created jobs of an acceptable quality and at an acceptable rate. It is likely that the usual conclusion would point to a need for a faster rate of job creation of a reasonable quality. This would generally require both faster growth and some changes in those factors susceptible to policy intervention that determine the employment outcomes of growth. The latter set of factors could be, in the order of the speed of their likely effectiveness: direct and publicly funded job-creation programmes; regulation and improvement of the terms and conditions of existing poor-quality jobs; manipulation of border prices and the allocation of credit to change the composition of output towards a pattern of labour demand that absorbs more, or a different category of, labour; building up supply-side factors, such as education and training; and overcoming discrimination and encouraging entrepreneurship. Supporters of a market liberalization approach would argue that aligning domestic and world relative prices and ensuring micro-level competition would lead to both faster growth and a faster rate of creation of reasonably good jobs by absorbing workers with the most common skills. However, all this would be meaningless in an economy beset with labour market rigidities because of discrimination and lack of opportunity. In addition, outcomes are likely to vary according to the concentration of asset ownership. Nevertheless, even when such structural features are set aside, there are likely to be many differences of opinion as to the areas of intervention (and the sequencing of such intervention) and how to assess the interaction of such action with overall growth. And, because the effects of some interventions are unknowable, there is also a premium on risk aversion, which finds its outlet in a cautious approach to policy change.

Given a good degree of equal opportunity and equal access to education, the substance of a common employment strategy can be seen in terms of two main elements: namely, achieving a high and sustained demand for labour and the flexibility (and the supporting policies and institutions) needed for workers to learn new skills and switch to working in new sectors and occupations (so that structural change does not disrupt employment levels). In addition, the distributional and participatory aspects of full employment should be second nature, an element perhaps not such much of an employment strategy but more of a general culture that rejects all forms of discrimination.

These aspects highlight the important role of social dialogue to forge agreements on new forms of labour market regulation in order to promote necessary levels of labour market flexibility as well as the need for minimum levels of social protection, assistance and safety nets to give some reassurance to those most likely to be negatively affected by change. The rejection of discrimination also suggests the value of an equal opportunity policy in the labour market as an incremental approach towards greater equality in general. Education and training are, therefore, important elements of an employment strategy, as are the anti-poverty, nutritional and gender programmes that allow them to be effective.

The interpretation of a "high and sustained" demand for labour is situation specific. It covers running economies at the highest possible level of nominal demand, consistent with both existing production capacity and sustaining investors' expectations of adding to existing capacity. Excessively high levels of nominal wage growth would affect these expectations. Measures also include preparing to take advantage of foreign demand through exporting, using semi-skilled workers, so long as this is consistent with labour standards, as well as infrastructure programmes (where appropriate, of a labour-intensive character), creating assets of general and beneficial use, thereby contributing to growth and employment. In a country with large numbers of relatively low-skilled, self-employed workers, this also means contributing to upgrading their resource base through credit programmes, well-chosen research and development, and other means of support consistent with encouraging the expansion of their activities.[27] In all these, active government policies are needed, as well as effective and honest administration. The policies chosen and the weight given to various elements in a mixture of policies need to be decided at national level.

In order to set certain parameters for the following chapters, the employment and labour market context of pursuing a full employment strategy and the main constraints to doing so are now examined for developing, industrialized and transition countries.

### Developing countries

A distinguishing characteristic of the labour markets in developing countries is that a large proportion of these countries' jobs is not found in the wage labour market: self-employed earners and unpaid family workers constitute a substantial part of employment.[28] Secondly, although there is much worker mobility between the wage and the non-wage sectors, there are many reasons why the rewards to workers are not equalized. An employment strategy will generally include two components, namely: (a) to increase income per earner in the non-wage sector and, thus, if possible, reduce the gap in income per earner between the wage and the non-wage sectors; and (b) to increase the proportion of employment in the *dynamic* parts of the wage sector, that is, move wage labour from the informal to the formal sectors (when the latter is competitive and able to survive without subsidies and protection).

In the literature of development economics dealing with poor, agrarian economies, the theory of "surplus labour" was advanced to describe the typical labour market situation in the rural sector. This surplus labour is not openly unemployed; it is absorbed in the family farm. Both work and income are shared out among the family members, so that the income of an adult worker in a family farm is similar to the *average* rather than the marginal product of labour. (In an enterprise, a worker's income is presumed to be equal to the marginal product.) But surplus need not mean idleness, and often, at low levels of income, many family members have to spend long hours at work trying to reach a tolerable level of income. Rather than idleness, surplus labour involves both a multiplicity of occupations for a typical worker and a hierarchy of earnings per hour in the different activities, with the earnings in the major activity (usually the cultivation of the major crop) being much higher than for other activities in home industry, trade and services. The existence of surplus labour implies that a great deal of the working time of rural workers is devoted to marginal activities with low earnings.

The co-existence of two broad sectors in the urban labour market, widely separated by their level of earnings unrelated to the human capital attributes of the workers, has already been emphasized. The high-wage sector is dominated by large firms or state-sector jobs, in which well-defined wage and employment contracts prevail. By contrast, the informal sector has flexible, albeit well-understood, work arrangements. The most important part of the informal sector is composed of self-employed small traders and businesses, but it also includes such large groups of people as casual day workers and wage earners in small enterprises, which are typically subject to little legal registration.[29] Two separate aspects of the formal/informal sector dichotomy are relevant to employment policy. The first concerns the causes of the earnings differential between the subsectors; the second, the degree of labour mobility from the informal to the formal sector.

In countries such as India, substantial wage differences in favour of large factories existed well before the coming of trade unions and labour legislation. The wage difference can be accounted for by the higher productivity of factories with their modern technology, giving capable workers opportunities to acquire new skills, and it is sustained by efficiency wage and profit-sharing considerations. The second aspect of labour market segmentation is the mobility of workers. Progress into the formal sector can be difficult or restricted. If this is generally true, it has serious implications for the distribution of income in the urban labour market. The wide difference in earnings between the two sectors, along with limited entry into the high-wage sector, creates an urban "labour aristocracy".[30] Labour mobility restrictions can arise from institutional factors. If employers attach more importance to the productivity-augmenting effects of a cohesive workforce than to getting in new workers at the lowest wage possible, they will then depend on supervisors and senior workers to help in recruitment. As a result, the selection of new recruits may be restricted to those people who have close kinship or community ties with already employed workers.

Segmentation can also occur when workers with different attributes are available in the job market. When these attributes are used as "labels" in the hiring of employees, the labour market may split up into non-competing groups, which sows the seeds of discrimination. The most important of these supply-side attributes are gender and education, while ethnic origin may also be important. (Such labelled, or statistical, segmentation is not, however, restricted to developing countries.) Achieving equal opportunity is, therefore, a matter of major concern.

The expansion of demand for labour in the wage sectors outside agriculture and the informal sector has traditionally been at the centre of attention of development strategies. Correspondingly, the State has usually provided the conditions for industrialization and thus the creation of high-productivity jobs, whether through a policy of import substitution or export orientation. Markets have rarely been left alone to make this choice, usually because of a lack of confidence in the ability of market forces to lead to socially desirable results in conditions where asset ownership is often highly concentrated. And the choice between these two approaches to industrialization has had significant implications for labour markets, with the second approach generally accepted as the more successful of the two (see Chapter 3). But there are limitations to pursuing a package of policies directed solely at expanding the demand for labour in the wage sector. If the reservoir of surplus labour in the subsistence agricultural sector is large – as is probably the case in the most populous Asian countries – it is extremely unlikely that employing more labour in the non-subsistence sector is going to raise labour earnings substantially in the former. Therefore, it is necessary to pursue the supplementary strategy of increasing the supply price of labour directly in the subsistence sector.

## *Industrialized countries*

Three substantial differences exist between the situation in industrialized and in developing countries. Firstly, there is much less intervention in economic structures on the part of governments in the former economies, reflecting the more efficient markets and the confidence in markets as the means of resource allocation. A general commitment to free trade (although with a number of quite serious exceptions in some sectors and activities) ensures a largely hands-off approach to structural change, which has been reinforced by 50 years of economic cooperation among industrialized countries and a commitment to abiding by the same rules of the game. This was exemplified by the industrialized countries agreeing to adopt the IMF's capital-account liberalization as an objective in 1997. There are, furthermore, many national practices and institutions in place that are aimed at making structural change socially acceptable. There may also be less need for government intervention in many aspects of economic life because bargaining between employers and workers can replace legislation on many facets of the employment relationship.

Secondly, there is the proliferation of income-support schemes in industrialized countries, principally for the unemployed, which serve both welfare and efficiency aims. These reflect the greater ease of resource mobilization in industrialized countries, that is, higher and more easily taxable incomes. The schemes also reflect an acceptance of a wider role for government and the development of a broader political base formed by those who can potentially benefit from transfers and redistribution.[31] The use of these schemes to intensify job search on the part of the unemployed – their "activation" – has become a major element of employment policies in industrialized countries. These schemes aid labour market efficiency by making it easier for round pegs to find round holes. However, income-support schemes may also mean that an unskilled, unemployed worker will, on accepting a job, only make a narrow income gain. Thus, the interaction of income taxation, social security and possible job subsidies in relation to decisions on jobseeking and acceptance is often complex and sometimes counter-productive.

The third dissimilarity lies in the depth of the capital markets in industrialized countries and hence the scope for government borrowing and deficit financing. This allows government intervention through the stimulation of the macroeconomy. (Developing countries can only do this to a significant extent by borrowing abroad, which is risky.) Consequently, an essential element in the framework for full employment in industrialized countries consists of running the macroeconomy to the full extent of its capacity and maximizing demand.[32] To do this successfully, of course, requires considerable judgement, taking inflation and balance-of-payment concerns and their effects on future investment into account. Wage behaviour and possible intervention and tripartite agreements in wage setting are extremely important in this respect. Given this macroeconomic background, an employment policy must fulfil two tasks: firstly, help all markets work effectively by removing trade, capital market and other distortions to increase competition; and, secondly, help individuals into work through skills upgrading and job counselling. Of course, there exist a number of different approaches to providing legislative help for workers in terms of job security and support for collective rather than individual action on the part of workers.

## Transition countries[33]

Whether transition economies can legitimately be considered a separate category, that is, neither developing nor industrialized, is debatable. The less wealthy transition economies of East and Central Asia have large agricultural sectors and thus share some of the attributes of developing countries. They can usefully follow policies that impinge directly on rural employment through, for example, increasing irrigation and improving agricultural practices. In Central and Eastern Europe, however, employment problems are much more an urban phenomenon and self-employment plays a much more limited role, although its potential may not yet have been reached. Few transition economies at any income level have the depth of capital markets that would allow substantial domestic government borrowing. To that extent, their internal freedom of action in ensuring full employment is less than that of industrialized countries, making them more similar to developing countries. But transition countries are, by and large, genuinely moving from a centralized to decentralized decision-taking process and away from government determination of the structure of production. Their transition status deprives them of several of the ways in which the goal of full employment can be pursued and of which industrialized countries can make use. Many of them have yet to establish either a competitive environment that can create jobs or the transparency and predictability of policy-making that can stimulate investment. To this extent, and hopefully only for a limited period, these countries are at a disadvantage, and so can be considered a separate case. However, they do share the labour market institutions and practices of industrialized countries in terms of assistance to the unemployed, social protection and social dialogue.

Aspects of employment policy, especially within the context of market liberalization and its advantages and drawbacks, will be revisited in Chapter 3. The next chapter reviews the current state of the world employment situation, looking at issues of both its quantity and quality.

## Notes

[1] For an account of the role of this Convention, see J. Mayer: "The employment policy convention: Scope, assessment and prospects", in *International Labour Review*, Vol. 130, No. 3, Geneva, 1991.

[2] As a rule, the ILO's supervisory body overseeing the implementation of ratified Conventions has had little to say in the past on the action taken by member countries. In the 1980s and 1990s, however, the supervisory body did level considerable criticism against some OECD member countries that had ratified the Convention. It was felt that, in some instances, the commitment to achieving full employment had been deliberately set aside and that some economic policies pursued to fulfil other objectives were not having a positive effect on employment levels. The customary government response to these charges has been to ask for more time to arrive at the Convention's objectives.

[3] The EU has a four-pillar strategy (employability, adaptability, entrepreneurship and equal opportunities) and, at the time of writing, 22 employment guidelines. Member countries draw up national action plans, which are monitored by the European Commission. However, there are some fears that the monitoring of this process is taking priority over actually achieving the desired result.

[4] Evidence for the spread of neo-liberalism would include the removal of restrictions on current-account transactions, imposed by some 60 per cent of the members of the International Monetary Fund (IMF) in 1987 but by only 18 per cent in early 2000, an increase in the ratio of trade to gross domestic product (GDP) – true for most developing countries – and a fall in the ratio of trade taxes to total trade.

[5] *Decent work*, Report of the Director-General, International Labour Conference, 87th Session, 1999.

[6] Many countries publish data from both sources. Administrative data are after all available for relatively compact geographical areas. Some countries, such as Germany, only carry out a labour force survey once a year, and otherwise refer to job registration data. But the drawback to using registration data is that they are neither compatible internationally nor often through time.

[7] Holding out for more attractive jobs is clearly a widespread phenomenon, and was highlighted in Dudley Seers' report for the ILO (*Matching employment opportunities and expectations: A programme of action for Ceylon*, Geneva, 1971). That it has not disappeared in that country is shown by M. Rama in *The Sri Lankan unemployment problem revisited*, World Bank Working Paper No. 2227 (Washington, DC, 1999). For an analysis of the Egyptian labour market, which reaches very similar conclusions, see R. Assaad: "The effects of public sector hiring and compensation policies on the Egyptian labour market", in *World Bank Economic Review*, Vol. 11, No. 1, Jan. 1997. A similar phenomenon apparently applies in southern Italy (see T. Boeri, R. Layard and S. Nickell: *Report to Prime Ministers Blair and D'Alema, Welfare to work and the fight against long-term unemployment*, 2000, available from: www.palazzochigi.it/approfondimenti/sindacati/inglese.html). In fact, in Sri Lanka, even in the early 1970s, this was not the whole story. Ranked by adult equivalence scales, the lowest quintile had the highest unemployed to population rate for men, and more of their unemployed were young. Unemployed to population ratios for women were similar for all income groups (see P. Richards and W. Gooneratne: *Basic needs, poverty and government policies in Sri Lanka*, Geneva, ILO, 1980).

[8] See *Concepts of labour force underutilization* (Geneva, ILO, 1971). Prepared by A. D. Smith, this report favoured household sample surveys collecting income and labour force data as allowing the widest form of analysis. A useful country comparison was made by P. Visaria: *Concepts and measurement of unemployment and underemployment in Asia and the Pacific: A comparative study*, Working Paper of the Asian Human Resource Development Planning Network (New Delhi, ILO, 1990).

[9] The use of this particular ratio, which aids international comparisons of employment levels, has been institutionalized as one of the indicators reported in the ILO publication, *Key Indicators of the*

*Labour Market* (Geneva, 1999). The range of indicators included for each country in this study taken together gives a good representation of a country's employment situation.

[10] See A. Berry and M. T. Mendez: *Policies to promote adequate employment in Latin America and the Caribbean*, ILO Employment and Training Working Paper, No. 46 (Geneva, 1999).

[11] A working definition of the informal sector in Latin America has usually included workers in very small enterprises (often five employees or fewer), most of the self-employed (excluding professional occupations) and domestic servants. This definition does not cover casual workers in larger size establishments.

[12] The European Commission has frequently floated ideas for a target employment rate of, for example, 70 per cent of the working-age population. The EU's Lisbon Summit of March 2000 agreed to this, in principle, as a goal for 2010, but still considered that targets should also be set nationally.

[13] D. Mazumdar: *Constraints to achieving full employment in Asia*, ILO Employment and Training Paper No. 51 (Geneva, 1999).

[14] Not that Arthur Lewis used the expression. He was concerned with the process of capital accumulation in the modern sector (see A. Lewis: "Economic development with unlimited supplies of labour", in *Manchester School of Economic and Social Studies*, Vol. XXII, No. 2, May 1954).

[15] A. K. Sen: "Work and rights", in *International Labour Review*, Vol. 139, 2000/2.

[16] "Drawing an income" as opposed to being totally independent and self-employed does presuppose an implicit or explicit employment relationship where the worker has rights, even if these are never fully specified (such as rights to an income as calculated in one way or another and rights to the enjoyment of certain conditions of work), and duties to the employer, the cooperative or the extended household. A major function of the ILO is to help clarify the form of these rights and duties as well as the means of their negotiation.

[17] Under the Emergency Powers (Defence) Act of 1940, the Government of the United Kingdom had the right to send national servicemen down the mines, known as the "direction of labour".

[18] The elimination of forced labour is one of the ILO's core principles. See the Forced Labour Convention, 1930 (No. 29).

[19] The freedom of action of the self-employed or of "independent" workers is usually very limited; in the most extreme cases are independent workers who are disguised (possibly subcontracted) wage workers, so that they are not so very different from wage workers.

[20] In the *Financial Times* (20 May 1999), R. Reich wrote, of the United States, that: "families are working far more hours to earn the same income: about six full-time working weeks' more than a decade ago". This claim, if applied to the population at large, appears valid for a somewhat longer period, that is, from 1983–98 when labour inputs rose by some 12 per cent (one-third longer hours, two-thirds higher employment to population rates). In the 1990s labour input growth was much lower, approximately 3 per cent, with much the same mix of contributory factors. Nonetheless, during the longer period, 40 per cent of the increase, it could be claimed, was actually caused by a fall in unemployment and was, presumably, welfare enhancing.

[21] The only wealthy countries with full employment and low growth are two oil-producing countries, Kuwait and Saudi Arabia. A major example of a country with badly distributed fast growth is China.

[22] D. Seers: "The Colombia employment programme", in *International Labour Review*, Vol. 102, No. 4, Oct. 1970.

[23] He wrote: "Even if it means slower economic growth, employment-oriented development is to be preferred on social grounds – so long as it does not result in actual economic stagnation." (See D. Morse: "The ILO World Employment Programme", in *International Labour Review*, Vol. 97, No. 6, June 1968.)

[24] In addition, forced labour should be forbidden and child labour permitted only under restricted conditions.

[25] Such as Gastil's civil liberties' index, which includes 14 items of individual and collective freedoms (see R. D. Gastil: *Freedom in the world*, Westport, CT, Greenwood, 1988).

[26] This is a particularly difficult issue to approach. On the one hand you have the "luxury unemployment" argument of G. Myrdal in *Asian drama* (Penguin, Harmondsworth/Pantheon, New

York, 1968), although this viewpoint was always an oversimplification. On the other you have the findings of, for example, Oswald, on the high levels of mental distress suffered by the unemployed, although even according to this criterion, the more educated apparently suffer more distress than the lesser educated (see A. Oswald: *Happiness and economic performance*, Warwick Economic Research Papers No. 478, Warwick University, United Kingdom, 1997).

[27] A good description of such needs is given in M. H. Khan: *Rural poverty in developing countries: Issues and policies*, IMF Working Paper, WP/00/78 (Washington, DC, 2000).

[28] This section draws heavily on Mazumdar (Geneva, ILO, 1999).

[29] Since attempts at regulation in Latin America have extended into the economy of the self-employed much more so than in Asia, the informal sector is also seen as a sector dominated by regulation evasion. However, the extent of compliance with regulations is related to an enterprise's size, location, capacity to pay, its judgement on the balance between the costs of compliance and the benefits it may bring, official capacity to enforce regulations and the enterprise's awareness of regulations. See V. Tokman and E. Klein (eds): *Regulation and the informal economy: Microenterprises in Chile, Ecuador and Jamaica* (Boulder, Colorado, Lynne Rienner Publishers, 1996).

[30] This is the stylized picture, which appears to break down in some middle-income countries. Thus, for Mexico, Maloney describes a situation of considerable movement between the informal and formal sectors, with wages sometimes more advantageous in the former (W. F. Maloney: *Are labour markets in developing countries dualistic?*, World Bank Working Paper No. 1941, Washington, DC, 1998). It is possible that blue-collar workers are limited in their prospects in larger enterprises and often prefer to leave for jobs in the informal sector. It is also possible that Mexico is atypical, since elsewhere in Latin America enterprise size is often found to influence earnings independent of characteristics such as age, gender and education.

[31] See S. Peltzman: "The growth of government", in *Journal of Law and Economics*, Vol. XXIII (2), Oct. 1980. Rodrik has linked the institution of wider redistributive programmes to the social acceptance of structural change (see D. Rodrik: *Has globalization gone too far?*, Institute for International Economics, Washington, DC, 1997).

[32] There is nothing new in this. In the preface to his book, *Lapses from full employment* (London, Macmillan, 1945), A. C. Pigou wrote that "Professor Denis Robertson has warned me that the form of the book may suggest that I am in favour of attacking the problem of unemployment by manipulating wages rather than by manipulating demand. I wish therefore to say clearly that this is not so." (Quoted in R. M. Solow: "On theories of unemployment", in *American Economic Review*, March 1980.)

[33] Includes the transition countries of East and Central Asia (Cambodia, China, Lao People's Democratic Republic, Mongolia and Viet Nam), the former centrally planned economies of Central Europe, and all parts of the former Soviet Union. In this study, the Commonwealth of Independent States (CIS) groups all the former Soviet Union countries, with the exception of the three Baltic States, and Central and Eastern Europe incorporates the former centrally planned economies of Central Europe and the European States of the CIS.

# THE CURRENT EMPLOYMENT PICTURE

# 2

## 2.1   Introduction

This chapter looks at the broad trends in employment and unemployment, paying particular attention to the years since the 1995 World Summit for Social Development. It also looks at the characteristics of employment quality, although they cannot be similarly quantified. Employment/unemployment trends are reviewed first globally, then regionally.

## 2.2   The global and regional employment picture

*An overview*

In Chapter 1 it was noted that different regions measure progress towards full employment and overcoming unemployment in different ways, and that the very range of average income levels prevailing across the world makes the interpretation and comparison of available data on employment and unemployment extremely difficult. Consequently, it is not usually possible to produce an aggregate picture of world employment. The aggregate numbers for employment or unemployment given in the media are not only statistically suspect but are also composed in such a way that any changes in the figures cannot be interpreted as showing a clear change in the welfare of workers.

Tables 2.1 and 2.2, which present and effectively compare data on employment and unemployment by region, are, of course, not exempt from such criticisms. For example, despite the figures given in table 2.1, the real level of unemployment in China is probably unknowable, since data on unemployment in rural areas, if collected, are not published. Data for

**Table 2.1**    Rates of unemployment and growth in numbers unemployed, by region, 1987–99

| Area/country | Unemployment rates | | | | | Percentage growth in numbers unemployed | | |
|---|---|---|---|---|---|---|---|---|
| | 1987 | 1993 | 1997 | 1998 | 1999 | 1987–97 | 1993–97 | 1993–99 |
| Developed countries | 7.6 | 8.2 | 7.4 | 7.1 | 6.8 | 0.7 | 1.1 | -0.2 |
| Europe | 10.4 | 10.6 | 10.3 | 9.7 | 9.2 | 1.1 | 2.9 | 0.2 |
| Japan | 2.8 | 2.5 | 3.4 | 4.1 | 4.7 | 2.9 | 7.8 | 11.1 |
| United States | 6.2 | 6.9 | 4.9 | 4.5 | 4.2 | -1.0 | -5.3 | -4.8 |
| Other developed countries (Australia, Canada, New Zealand) | 8.3 | 11.0 | 8.8 | 8.1 | 7.4 | 2.0 | -3.6 | -3.9 |
| Latin America and the Caribbean | 5.7[1] | 6.1 | 7.2 | 8.0 | 8.7[2] | 7.3[3] | n.a. | n.a. |
| China | 2.0 | 2.6 | 3.1 | 3.1 | n.a. | 0.1 | 7.3 | 6.5[5] |
| India | 3.8 | 2.3 | n.a. | n.a. | n.a. | n.a. | n.a. | n.a. |
| Other countries in Asia | 3.7 | 3.9 | 4.9 | 5.8 | n.a. | 1.6 | 0.8 | n.a. |
| Central Europe[4] | – | 14.0 | 11.9 | 12.6 | 15 6 | – | -3.9 | -2.1[5] |
| CIS | – | 3.6 | 7.6 | 8.5 | 8.5[6] | – | 19.8 | 19.3[5] |

n.a. = figures not available; – = nil or negligible.

Notes:    [1]1990. [2]Data from the Economic Commission for Latin America and the Caribbean (CEPAL): *Panorama social de América Latina, 1999–2000* (Santiago, 2000). This source gives a figure of 8.1 per cent for 1998. The ILO gives a figure of 8 per cent for the first quarter of 1999. The data refer only to urban areas. [3]1990–97. [4]Data for Central Europe exclude the Baltic States, which had a total of 270,000 unemployed in 1998. [5]1993–98. [6]Author's estimates based on partial regional data.

Calculations are based on labour force surveys (for developed countries and other countries in Asia), household surveys and official data (Central Europe and the CIS, Latin America and the Caribbean) or national sources (China, India). No comprehensive data for Africa are available.

Sources:    ILO: *Yearbook of Labour Statistics* (Geneva, various years), and *Informa: Panorama laboral* (Lima, various years); OECD: *Employment Outlook* and *Labour Force Statistics* (Paris, various years); Economic Commission for Europe (ECE): *Economic Survey of Europe* (Geneva, various years).

"other countries in Asia" are a population-weighted average of a number of countries in which three – Bangladesh, Indonesia and Pakistan – predominate. It would be an interesting and useful exercise to check the comparability of their means of data collection, methodology and questions used in gathering information on women's work, etc., since these are probably not consistent. The unemployment rate does show a sharp rise in 1998, although there had previously been an upward trend. Other data are no doubt generally accurate in the sense that they faithfully reflect the methodology used. Table 2.1 suggests that a population-weighted world unemployment rate was not particularly high (in the range of 4–5 per cent) in the period 1997–98. It could also be said to have been relatively stable throughout most of the 1990s, that is, with the fall in the rate for developed countries cancelling out the rise in Central Europe, the CIS, "other

**Table 2.2.** Growth rates of employment, labour productivity and the labour force, 1987–99 (as a percentage)

| Area/country | 1987–97 | | 1993–97 | | 1993–99 | | Labour force | | |
|---|---|---|---|---|---|---|---|---|---|
| | E | LP | E | LP | E | LP | 1987–97 | 1993–97 | 1993–99 |
| Developed countries | 1.1 | 1.3 | 1.0 | 1.3 | 1.1 | 1.4 | 1.1 | 0.8 | 0.8 |
| Europe | 0.9 | 1.9 | 0.4 | 2.3 | 0.8 | 1.9 | 0.9 | 0.3 | 0.5 |
| Japan | 1.0 | 1.5 | 0.4 | 1.5 | neg. | -0.1 | 1.1 | 0.6 | 0.4 |
| United States | 1.4 | 1.0 | 1.9 | 0.8 | 1.7 | 1.4 | 1.3 | 1.3 | 1.2 |
| Other developed countries (Australia, Canada and New Zealand) | 1.3 | 1.1 | 2.0 | 1.3 | 1.8 | 1.3 | 1.4 | 1.4 | 1.4 |
| Latin America and the Caribbean | $2.8^1$ | $0.3^1$ | n.a. | n.a. | n.a. | n.a. | $3.1^1$ | n.a. | n.a. |
| China | $1.0^4$ | 10.0 | n.a. | n.a. | n.a. | n.a. | $1.5^2$ | $1.1^3$ | n.a. |
| India | $2.4^5$ | 2.7 | n.a. | n.a. | n.a. | n.a. | 2.2 | n.a. | n.a. |
| Other countries in Asia | $2.0^6$ | 6.6 | 2.4 | $4.5^3$ | n.a. | n.a. | $1.9^6$ | $2.3^3$ | n.a. |
| Central Europe[7] | -1.5 | 1.0 | neg. | 4.3 | neg. | $3.3^8$ | -0.6 | -0.5 | $-0.2^8$ |
| CIS | -1.0 | -2.9 | -1.5 | -3.7 | $-1.4^8$ | $-2.9^8$ | -0.3 | -0.5 | $-0.4^8$ |

E = employment; LP = labour productivity; n.a. = figures not available; neg. = negligible.
Notes:  [1]1990–98. [2]1987–96. [3]1993–96. [4]1990–97. [5]1987–93. [6]1990–96. [7]Excludes the Baltic States. [8]1993–98.
Sources:  See table 2.1.

countries in Asia" and Latin America. But it should be stressed that, for example, an unemployment rate of 4 per cent in the United States represents a far tighter labour market and a higher associated growth of high-quality jobs than a lower unemployment rate in India or Indonesia. The numbers unemployed grew particularly fast in the mid- to late 1990s in Japan and the CIS. The relatively fast growth of the numbers unemployed in China reflects the fast growth of the urban labour force.

In Central Europe and the CIS in the period 1987–97 employment fell by more than the fall in the labour force, and in Latin America and the Caribbean employment rose by less than the rise in the labour force, as table 2.2 shows. The situation for Central Europe subsequently changed. In Asia, employment grew generally faster than the labour force. Table 2.2 also gives data on labour productivity growth (that is, total output divided by employment). In the United States until 1997 the relatively low labour productivity growth rates, by comparison with Europe, are associated with fast employment growth. It is of major importance to investigate the possible trade-off between these two outcomes and subsequent developments (see Chapter 3). China is clearly the star performer, followed by "other countries in Asia". India also experienced relatively high labour productivity growth in the early 1990s. The performance of Latin America and the Caribbean and the CIS in terms of productivity growth was poor. Central

Europe in the mid- to late 1990s saw employment stabilizing as well as a rise in labour productivity.

If the global unemployment rate changed little throughout the 1990s, it follows that employment grew broadly as fast as the labour force. How labour force growth has related to population growth depends on the balance between a general trend of higher labour force participation rates for women and falling rates for men. A part of the former may represent only a growing recognition of women's contribution to output and not a real change in their activities. And there is no doubt that the global labour force participation rate of women still remains underestimated.

It is worthwhile stepping back and looking at the global employment situation in a longer-term perspective. Unfortunately, the only available statistics are rather unhelpful, relating as they do to employment in very broad sectoral categories, such as agriculture and manufacturing (single-digit ISIC 2 classification). Slightly more detail is available for industrialized countries, in which services are separated into personal and social (government, education, health, etc.) sectors. For Latin America, composite estimates of employment in domestic services are also available. Such broad categories can only suggest certain changes in employment quality. It is assumed here that the nature of employment in some of these sectors is more likely to be a cause of concern than in others, that is, on the negative, weaker side you have employment in agriculture, trade, hotels and restaurants and most personal services and, on the positive, stronger side, are jobs in manufacturing, utilities, banking, finance and government and community services. The former group is more likely to consist of more isolated work in small groups as well as part-time work (usually undertaken by women), where workers have greater difficulty in organizing themselves to protect their interests. Incomes also tend to fluctuate more in these sectors. The unemployed, especially in industrialized countries, should also be added to this group. (In other countries the potential unemployed are included in one of the low-employment quality sectors.) It should be noted that two major sectors – transport and construction – do not feature in either group.

From the 1920s and 1930s to the 1970s the fall in the share of employment in the weaker sectors in the major industrialized countries was often around 20 percentage points (in France, for example, between 1921 and 1971 the share of employment fell from 56 to 35 per cent). The rise in the stronger sectors was substantial but usually somewhat less dramatic (in Italy, for example, between 1921 and 1961 the employment share rose from 25 to 39 per cent). After about 1970 and taking unemployment into account, the situation began to change: the size of the weaker segment rose (at least until the early 1990s) and that of the stronger segment fell or stagnated.[1] Obviously, higher unemployment and lower employment levels in manufacturing combined to generate what is more or less the employment picture today (see the section on Western Europe, North America and Australasia) – one of some ambiguity, with a growth of both high- and low-quality jobs, more temporary work but little change in most workers' job duration. There is also believed to have been a rise in many workers' feelings of insecurity. It is possible that this is related as much or more to changes in the nature and intensity of work (greater employer control, fewer promotion prospects under new forms of work organization) and to a reduced level of in-work benefits as to the risk of job loss.

Between 1960 and 1980, the picture in Latin America was similar; employment in the weaker sectors fell by some 10 percentage points and that in the stronger sectors rose (by about 7 percentage points). Like in the industrialized countries, the situation changed, but this time after 1980. The share in the weaker segment continued to fall, but the share in the stronger segment also fell. (Consequently, growth in transport and construction, where employment might be either formal or informal, rose.) In 1980, the share of employment in manufacturing reached its peak – at around 18 per cent (low by historical standards) – and subsequently fell to around 13 per cent. Government services hardly increased. Agriculture, meanwhile, fell from nearly 50 per cent of employment in 1960 to under 20 per cent by the end of the 1990s.[2]

However, the experience of Latin America after 1980 would not appear to be typical for developing countries in general. Changes in the structure of employment, which are obviously associated with changes in the structure of GDP, are not wholly predictable. They respond both to per capita growth rates and, in ways that might not always be expected, to initial per capita income levels. Taking first total male employment in a sample of 20 developing countries in the 1980s, the usual pattern was a sizeable fall in agriculture and a slight rise in trade, restaurants, etc.[3] This net fall in poorer-quality jobs was largely offset by a rise in manufacturing, financial services and government and community services jobs. On balance the weaker segment fell and the stronger rose, that is, they displayed the same pattern as the industrialized countries prior to 1970. The fall in the share of agriculture was greatest in the fastest-growing countries, irrespective of their initial income level. The rise in employment in trade, restaurants, etc., was also greater in faster-growing as well as in higher-income countries (that is, employment in these sectors inevitably replaces some of the fall in agricultural employment, increasingly so as per capita incomes rise). The share of manufacturing employment for men did not respond to faster growth at all. Employment in financial services rose quickest in higher-income countries, more or less irrespective of their rate of growth, and employment in the construction and transport sectors responded principally to rates of growth. Male employment in government and community services rose quickest in the lower-income countries.

The same exercise was carried out for women workers and was divided between countries where data on total female employment were felt to be reliable (broadly in Asian countries) and those where only the data on female wage employment seemed acceptable. Taking the latter (wage employment) first, structural changes in employment seemed highly favourable, that is, there were substantial gains in manufacturing and in financial services and, to a lesser degree, in government and community services. In both the first two sectors, employment growth responded favourably to per capita income growth. Female wage employment would thus seem to benefit from faster growth. However, what happens to female non-wage employment is less clear. The picture for total female employment in Asian countries was less favourable than for wage employment, although the pattern was similar. Employment in the weaker segments of the labour market fell – by some 3 percentage points – and that in stronger sectors rose – by over 2 percentage points. In fact, the picture for all female workers was broadly similar to that for all men.

These trends in the 1980s were in tune with the earlier experience of the industrialized countries. By and large the share of apparently better (i.e., stronger-sector) jobs rose and that of probably worse (weaker-sector) jobs fell. One caveat, however, is that only one sub-Saharan African country was included in the sample. Following the analysis into the 1990s, using countries outside Latin America is not easy, and no sub-Saharan African country could be included in the sample. Broadly speaking, the share of employment in agriculture for both men and women continued to fall. Employment in manufacturing often fell or stagnated, especially for men. The share of employment in trade, restaurants, etc., rose almost universally, but not by as much as the drop in agricultural employment. The share of jobs presumed to be of low quality thus continued to fall. By and large the share of employment in government and community services rose sufficiently to offset the frequent stagnation in manufacturing.

As a result the Latin American picture of a fall in the share of high-quality jobs in the 1990s was not repeated elsewhere (the data predominantly relate to Asia). Generally, however, the fall in apparently low-quality jobs continued to be greater than the rise in apparently high-quality jobs, which makes it difficult to judge the final outcome. Finally, on this basis, the apparent quality of women's employment improved faster than that of men's.

*Central and Eastern Europe[4]*

Central and Eastern Europe is increasingly becoming two sub-regions. Some Central European countries are members of the OECD and, more importantly, are lining up to join the EU. It is not certain whether EU membership will create either prosperity or full employment, but it should result in a harmonization of many terms and conditions of employment and other features, which should raise job quality. Large parts of the CIS, however, and above all the Russian Federation (despite the beneficial effects of a large devaluation and high oil prices) and Ukraine, are, currently, in unsustainable positions of considerable economic instability. Since 1995, the gap, especially, between the Russian Federation and Ukraine and countries bordering the EU has widened. Employment performance in Central Europe overall is scarcely satisfactory; unemployment, for example, has been increasing rapidly in the Czech Republic and Slovakia, and indeed in 1999 rose nearly everywhere. Completing the agenda of structural change in these countries may push employment down even further. The unemployment position of the larger countries of Eastern Europe or the CIS, where output is stagnant at best and wage arrears are substantial, has generally been deteriorating since 1995 (see table 2.3).

What all the countries in table 2.3 had in common before the collapse of communism were the institutions and mechanisms that found a job for everyone who wanted one and indeed put pressure on most of those in the relevant age groups to take a job. Wages were purposely set low, so that nearly all adults had to work, and the enjoyment of the benefits of the social security system was closely attached to employment status. Enterprises were not pressurized to take on workers but deliberately chose to do so because a larger workforce usually gave managers more power and prestige. Women were educated to work, and usually opted to do so since one salary per family was rarely sufficient, and later their education levels exceeded men's. Childcare facilities were established, although (despite original plans to "liberate" women from household chores) practically no other services were provided on a communal basis and women had little choice but to go out to work, look after the household and the children.[5]

With the 1990s came some drastic changes. The transition process began, in most countries, with a substantial fall in output as economic and political factors interacted negatively. The former Soviet Union split up, the Council for Mutual Economic Assistance (Comecon) was dissolved, prices and foreign trade were liberalized, central planning was removed and, because of high levels of foreign debt, some of the countries began the new era with austerity policies. Price decontrol opened the way for prices

**Table 2.3**   Unemployment in Central and Eastern Europe, 1995 and 1999 (as a percentage)

| Country | 1995 | 1999 | |
|---|---|---|---|
| Albania | 12.9 | 18.0[1] | |
| Belarus | 2.7 | 2.0 | |
| Bulgaria | 11.1 | 16.0 | |
| Croatia | 17.6 | 20.8 | |
| Czech Republic | 2.9 | 9.4 | |
| Hungary | 10.4 | 9.6 | (7.0 LFS) |
| Poland | 14.9 | 13.0 | (12.5 LFS)[2] |
| Romania | 9.5 | 11.5 | (6.9 LFS) |
| Russian Federation | 8.9 | 12.3 | |
| Slovakia | 13.1 | 19.2 | |
| Ukraine | 1.5 | 4.3 | |

LFS = labour force survey.
Notes:    [1]Second quarter of 1999. [2]February 1999.
There is, unfortunately, no convincing reason to have much faith in either the level or direction of these figures. They are data on registered job applicants and the numbers can rise or fall for seemingly arbitrary administrative reasons. Labour force survey data are better guides to unemployment levels and increasingly exist. They do not, however, go back many years. For Central Europe and the Baltic States, labour force survey numbers of the unemployed are generally lower, often considerably so, than those registered unemployed. The figure given in the table for the Russian Federation (12.3) is an estimate given by its statistical office, based on data from a survey of establishments, not households. By contrast, registered unemployment in late 1999 was under 2 per cent.
Source:    ECE: *Economic Survey* (Geneva, 2000).

to rise and inflation often rose because of excessive monetary expansion. At the same time, new opportunities opened up: in the services sector (which has usually expanded its employment share); in self-employment (which was next to zero in many countries under the old system); and in small-scale enterprises. The fall in output would have implied a fall in wage levels even if the distribution of income had remained steady; in fact, income distribution appears to have universally worsened. This can only partly be attributed to a change in wage differentials rewarding human capital (in the CIS countries industrial wage differentials remain in favour of commodity-exporting sectors). The worsening of income distribution is also, on the one side, a result of the proliferation of profitable and semi-legal authorities and, on the other, of a weakening position in the labour force for many workers and their families. In most countries, labour force participation rates fell rapidly, especially for women, and for younger and older people. Employment levels declined, with some workers leaving the labour force and others becoming unemployed. Unemployment rose from the very low levels (if at all) of the end of the 1980s, as has the prevalence of people holding two jobs.

Clearly, when viewed on the same terms as developed market economies, the countries of Central and Eastern Europe are far from achieving full employment. Only Poland and the Czech Republic appear to have had any real wage growth over a period of years (others have had irregular wage growth or growth only after a long, drawn-out decline in real wages); only in Poland and Hungary do open unemployment levels appear to have been falling. And where countries such as Ukraine have, on the surface, low unemployment rates, when part-time workers and workers sent on administrative leave (who keep a non-working connection with the enterprise) are included in the figures, the real unemployment rate becomes a multiple of the apparent rate. Finally, newly recruited workers are often offered fixed- and short-term contracts, the antithesis of the earlier "right to work".

The varying experiences of the larger countries can be summarized as follows: between 1990 and 1998 GDP in the Russian Federation fell by over 40 per cent, yet total employment fell by less than 15 per cent and official estimates of unemployment show that it rose to only 12 per cent. In Ukraine, the pattern was similar: the collapse of GDP (by 60 per cent) was even greater than in the Russian Federation, but official unemployment remained almost negligible, although industrial employment declined in the period 1992–95 by almost one-third. Official unemployment figures probably remained so low mainly because of the growth of the unofficial economy. It is notable, too, that (official) self-employment remains very limited and that most of those leaving industrial employment seem to have done so voluntarily.

By contrast, in the Czech Republic employment fell little (around 7 per cent in seven years) and unemployment has long remained almost negligible. After an initial jump in 1991, registered unemployment stabilized at around 3 per cent in 1992–96, but has since risen substantially (see table 2.3). Economy-wide labour productivity growth was relatively rapid in 1993–97, averaging around 2.5 per cent per year. In Slovakia, the fall in employment was much larger and its recovery much weaker than in the Czech Republic, and unemployment has been much higher. (This has also been the pattern in Bulgaria.) In 1991, registered unemployment rose in the space of six months from 2 per cent to 13 per cent, and until recently had remained broadly at that level. Labour force participation also fell by about 5 per cent during the period 1989-96, with an even larger decrease in female participation rates. On the other hand, since 1995 employment in Slovakia has been growing at around 2 per cent per annum.

Despite the big differences in unemployment experience between the Czech Republic and Slovakia, the path of real wages has been very similar in the two countries. Both countries saw a sharp fall in real consumption wages in 1990–91, followed by a period of sustained growth. Slovakia experienced the bigger drop (of about 28 per cent) and a slower recovery, and by 1997 real wages were still about 5 per cent below their 1990 level. In the Czech Republic, a somewhat smaller fall and a stronger recovery put real wages in 1997 about 5 per cent above their 1990 level.

In Hungary, the recession of the early 1990s resulted in huge job losses; employment fell by no less than 25 per cent between 1990 and 1995 and then turned modestly upward. Unemployment peaked at around 12 per cent in 1992, since when it has stabilized at around 10 per cent. Real wages have been relatively stable, in marked contrast to the impressive growth in labour productivity. Overall productivity, measured by GDP per employee, grew by 3.9 per cent per year in the period 1990–98. Since real wages in terms of producer prices fell slightly in the same period, the resulting positive gap between labour productivity and real producer wage growth indicates a fall in unit labour costs, which may well have played a large part in explaining the attraction of Hungary to domestic and foreign investors; investment in the country rose considerably throughout the period.[6]

In Poland, following the "big bang" of 1990, the unemployment rate jumped from virtually zero to around 12 per cent in 1991, rising to a peak of 16 per cent in 1993 (by a large margin the highest rate outside the Balkans) and falling only slowly thereafter. In addition to the increase in numbers unemployed, a roughly equal number of people of working age left the labour force. The combined effect meant that, between 1991 and 1994, employment relative to the population of working age fell from 78 per cent to 66 per cent. After 1994, sustained growth in the economy helped reduce unemployment gradually, but in 1997 it was still over 10 per cent. As Poland is easily the best performer of all the transition countries in growth of GDP and industrial production, it is scarcely surprising that total employment fell little in 1990–92 and recovered strongly thereafter. However, the employment level in 1997 was below that of 1990, so the overall picture was one of "jobless growth".

In Romania, relative employment stability in 1990–94 was bought at the cost of a 36 per cent fall in consumption wages. When employment levels subsequently began to fall, real wages rebounded by about one-third. But this large increase contributed to the need for a policy reversal in 1997, and another major fall in real wages took place. In Bulgaria, the fall in real wages reached 28 per cent by 1997, although the rate of decline was slowing by the end of the period.

In short, there have been considerable differences in the transition experiences of these countries. The Russian Federation has allowed open unemployment to emerge on a far larger scale than has Ukraine. Hungary experienced a far greater fall in employment than did Poland. By 1998, both Slovakia and the Czech Republic had both more or less returned to their 1990 GDP levels, although unemployment levels in Slovakia were double those of the Czech Republic.

## Asia[7]

Before the 1995 World Summit for Social Development and until the onset of the Asian financial crisis in 1997, some Asian countries and territories, mainly those in East and South-East Asia, were making steady progress towards full employment, while others were barely managing to maintain the status quo. In the Republic of Korea, Malaysia, Singapore and Hong Kong (China), employment growth consistently outpaced labour force growth, and unemployment declined to very low levels. Labour shortages arose and many countries hosted large numbers of migrant workers (up to 20 per cent of the labour force in Malaysia; higher in Singapore). The incidence of poverty fell to insignificant levels in the course of a decade. In Indonesia and the Philippines, however, employment growth failed to keep pace with labour force growth, and unemployment tended to rise. Both countries became major exporters of workers – by 1998 an estimated six million Filipinos were working outside the Philippines (of whom probably more than half were women) and over two million Indonesians were working abroad. Compared with the Philippines, incomes in Indonesia had been growing faster since the 1980s and its migrant workers are usually less skilled than Filipino migrant workers.

The generally positive employment trends in Asia have recently become tarnished. After many years of healthy growth, Japan continues in recession; its economy contracted by 2.5 per cent in 1998 and appears to have stagnated in 1999; its unemployment rate rose from 3.4 per cent in 1997 to 4.7 per cent in 1999.

But the largest and most serious reversal of positive employment trends was caused by the Asian crisis of late 1997, the effects of which are, in some countries, still apparent. In Indonesia, for example, GDP fell by 15 per cent in 1998 and stagnated in 1999; the ILO has estimated that between 3.8 million and 5.4 million workers were made redundant. Moreover, Indonesian migrant workers returned home in large numbers, especially from Malaysia. However, neither of these groups would necessarily have been reflected in increased unemployment levels, which nonetheless reached 5.5 per cent in 1998 (compared with 4.0 per cent in 1996). The reason for this is that most of these workers would have been forced to find a few hours' work a week on farms or with small businesses, which, as has been discussed in Chapter 1, would lead them to being classified as employed in labour force surveys. The incidence of poverty is thought to have more than doubled from the 11 per cent recorded in 1997, and the poor simply do not have the savings needed to tide them over bad patches. In Thailand, GDP declined by nearly 10 per cent in 1998. The effects on employment were already evident by early 1998 and suggested a fall in total labour inputs (a rise in unemployment, a fall in hours worked) by 7 to 8 per cent. The rate of open unemployment increased from 2.2 per cent to 4.8 per cent (February 1997–February 1998).[8] Real wages fell by some 10 per cent from late 1997 to early 1998, and self-employment earnings may have fallen further. In both Indonesia and Thailand women and men appear to have been affected to a similar degree.

In the Republic of Korea, real wages of regular employees fell by 12 per cent from the end of 1997 to early 1999, when they began to rise again. In the same period, the unemployment rate for women rose from 2.3 per cent to 5.8 per cent and that for men from 2.8 per cent to 8.1 per cent. Overall employment declined by around 5 per cent for both sexes, but the decline in the number of regular employees was greater for women (nearly 15 per cent) than for men (9 per cent). There is evidence that the informal sector is growing and that more workers, especially women, are cramming into the already overstaffed retail sector. In the Philippines, employment conditions have shown signs of a sharp deterioration and open unemployment may have reached 9.6 per cent in 1998, compared with 7.4 per cent in 1996. The average real wage declined by 3 per cent during 1998.

By mid-1999 the employment situation in the region was becoming slightly clearer. In the Republic of Korea, unemployment was down some 2 per cent over the previous year – to 6.5 per cent (and fell to 4 per cent by mid-2000). However, unemployment rates rose in Hong Kong (China) from 2.2 per cent in 1997 to 5.7 per cent in early 2000, and in otherwise scarcely affected Malaysia (up to 4.5 per cent in early 1999 from 2.5 per cent in 1997; they fell to 3 per cent at the end of 1999). Quite possibly a "ratchet" effect has taken place, with unemployment rates higher than before, despite a revival of economic growth.

Largely because of controls on foreign borrowing, the countries of South Asia were not so affected by the Asian financial crisis and, since 1995, employment growth has largely kept pace with labour force growth. This has, of course, meant more self-employment and casual labour in absolute terms. Regular wage employment in the modern sector is, however, currently declining, and there have been some signs of redundancy. The share of agriculture in total employment has declined only slowly. Open unemployment has been low, except in Sri Lanka (where it is slowly declining, falling from 14 per cent in 1993 to 9 per cent in 1999). The incidence of poverty in South Asia, though falling, remains high. The migration of workers for employment overseas has emerged as an important feature in Bangladesh, Pakistan and Sri Lanka.

The main factor behind the steady progress towards full employment of much of East and South-East Asia before the crisis had been the region's rapid economic growth. But even this had not always been sufficient to create jobs on the scale needed. China's growth rate was higher than that of Thailand, and Indonesia's growth rate only slightly below it; yet only Thailand achieved substantial progress towards full employment, probably because it had less underemployment than the other countries.

Meanwhile, taken from a global perspective, the growth rates of the South Asian countries have by no means been negligible. There is much anecdotal evidence that their employment situation has improved in certain dimensions, including through higher wages in rural areas, but, because of irregular data collection and long delays in data processing, hard facts are lacking.

The most likely explanation for the different employment experiences in Asia before the financial crisis may be the variety of labour policies the different countries pursued. In the transition economies of Asia and in South Asia (and, indeed, in West Asia), labour policies appear to have generated significant rigidities in the organized labour market, with bureaucratic methods of labour allocation and the responsibility of enterprises for providing social services to their workers severely restricting labour mobility. In East and South-East Asia, however, labour regulations did not obstruct labour reallocation and, by the 1980s, wages were rising in step with productivity. (Furthermore, in the mid-1990s, both Indonesia and Thailand instigated significant rises in the minimum wage.) Nevertheless, major gaps in the governance of the labour market existed, in particular those concerning freedom of association, a state of affairs that is often linked to the absence of government accountability in some parts of South-East Asia.

Historically, the situation in China bears some resemblance to what was going on in Central and Eastern Europe. Before 1978, all jobseekers were assigned either to local communes in rural areas, or to urban work units. The matching was bureaucratic and mandatory, and usually permanent. Even when this system ended, public authorities at all levels continued to exert pressure on enterprises to absorb workers, and only in the mid-1990s did managers acquire the power to dismiss surplus workers.[9]

The overall employment picture in China is summarized in table 2.4, which shows that between 1990–98 the labour force rose by 60.5 million. However, rural farm activities accounted for a much smaller number of the total at the end of the period, which implies that some 83 million workers were absorbed elsewhere. In the whole 1990–98 period, township and village enterprises (TVEs) absorbed about 40 per cent of these workers, private enterprise took 31 per cent and rising unemployment about 12 per cent. However, after 1997 employment levels in TVEs apparently failed to expand and the private sector became the largest incremental employer. Employment in state and collective enterprises fell substantially in 1998, and if workers continue to be "furloughed" (that is, given leave of absence) from state enterprises, the private sector will have to expand quickly to prevent unemployment from rising and to absorb rural workers.[10] On the basis of table 2.4 it would appear that this is hardly possible and that the category of people employed in "other rural activities" began to expand in number again in 1998 after a period of decline. By the mid-1990s, the share of superfluous workers had become very large, believed to be up to 30 per cent in state enterprises, 20 per cent in state and urban collective enterprises and the same share in TVEs. In urban areas, surplus workers have for some years been shunted into subsidiary companies, but more recently enterprises have been permitted to send workers on leave on more or less half wages. Usually these workers are older, female and the poorer educated. Official unemployment figures, which refer only to legal urban residents and exclude all rural residents and migrants (who are not allowed to register as unemployed), are apparently around 3 per cent (as shown in table 2.1) to which the share of "furloughed" workers who are genuinely available for work should be added. (Table 2.1 assumes this could bring the unemployment rate in urban areas up to between 6 and 6.5 per cent in the late 1990s.) Given these estimates of worker redundancy, it would seem that the fall in employment in 1998 in state and collective enterprises and TVEs was just a beginning. It can also be questioned whether the apparent dichotomy between "formal urban" and the implicitly "informal rural" accords with the facts.

Since 1995 and in line with earlier trends of fast economic growth, real wages in China appear to have risen substantially, although wage differentials have increased. Poverty has continued to fall, although in recent years the rate of decline has been far faster in urban than in rural areas, reflecting an urban bias in investment and in economic policy in general.[11] Indeed, from 1985–95 the annual rate of reduction in the number of the poor in

**Table 2.4**   China: Labour force, 1980–98 (in millions)

| Labour force by activity | 1980 | 1990 | 1997 | 1998 |
|---|---|---|---|---|
| *Urban areas* | | | | |
| Employed in state enterprises[1] | 80.2 | 103.5 | 110.4 | 90.6 |
| Employed in collectives[2] | 24.2 | 35.5 | 28.8 | 19.6 |
| Employed in other enterprises[3] | 0.0 | 1.6 | 11.1 | 16.7 |
| Employed in private enterprises | 0.8 | 6.7 | 26.7 | 32.3 |
| Total urban employment | 105.2 | 166.2[4] | 202.1[4] | 206.8[4] |
| Urban unemployed | 5.2 | 4.2 | 14.1 | 14.1 |
| Urban labour force | 110.4 | 170.4 | 216.2 | 220.9 |
| *Rural areas* | | | | |
| Employed in TVEs | 30.0 | 92.6 | 130.5 | 125.4 |
| Employed in other rural activities | 283.2 | 376.1 | 349.3 | 353.3 |
| Total rural labour force | 313.2 | 468.7 | 479.8 | 478.7 |
| Total labour force | 423.6 | 639.1 | 696.0 | 699.6 |

TVEs = township and village enterprises (*xiangzhen qiye*).

Notes:   [1]State sector: firms "owned by all the people" (*quanmin suoyouzhi*) and responsible to the central government. Many state firms operate under the direction of provincial or city governments. [2]Collective firms (*jiti suoyouzhi*), like state firms, are part of the public sector. They report to local authorities rather than to the central government. The collective sector includes urban enterprises and rural firms, known as TVEs, that operate under the supervision of local governments in rural areas. [3]Firms outside the state and collective sectors are often combined into the heterogeneous category of "Other" ownership (*qita suoyouzhi*). This table breaks this category into two components, namely "other", which are generally foreign-owned or foreign joint ventures or establishments with state participation, and "private", which refers to domestically owned, private enterprises. [4]Total exceeds sum of components (source provides no explanation for this discrepancy).

Sources:   *China Statistical Yearbook: People's Republic of China* (various years).

rural areas was under 1 per cent, compared with 6 per cent in urban areas – despite a general rise in food prices relative to the overall cost of living which should have been to the relative benefit of rural areas. The rural/urban exodus has continued, despite official discouragement, and many rural migrants are employed as casual workers in urban enterprises on relatively unfavourable terms. As noted, the focus of new employment creation has shifted from TVEs to the incipient private sector, and pressures arising from market liberalization have resulted in a gradual commercialization of the demand for labour, even within the state sector, with obviously both positive elements (reversing inflexibility in labour use) and negative elements (growing insecurity for the workforce). Women have been negatively affected by the smaller number of services being provided collectively by enterprises. There is now more mobility, turnover and flexibility in wages and terms of employment and largely greater scope for private business. But this goes hand in hand with far greater continuing official support for urban rather than rural workers.

In West Asia, open unemployment has apparently been increasing in recent years.[12] Certainly, it appears that labour migration within the region (mainly male), which acted as a major safety value in the 1980s, had levelled off even before the 1990–91 Gulf crisis. Unemployment rates have been variously estimated for the mid- to late 1990s as 6 per cent in the Syrian Arab Republic, 12 per cent in Yemen, 17 per cent in Jordan, 33 per cent in Iraq and from 18 to 51 per cent in the West Bank and Gaza. In the Islamic Republic of Iran the unemployment rate in the early 1990s fell to 11 per cent (down from 15 per cent in the mid-1980s), although the figures were three times as high for women as for men. (Generally, some two-thirds of the unemployed are aged between 15 and 24.)

In most of these countries the labour force situation of women differs markedly from that of men, although some of the differences that show up in the statistics may reflect prejudice in reporting rather than fact. In country after country in the Middle East, data show that the share of women aged 25–54 who are "economically inactive" (that is, reported as neither employed nor unemployed, but, even if this is correct, are no doubt working hard in other ways) is in the 65–80 per cent range, compared with rates for men that never exceed 5 per cent.[13] This is all the more surprising since there has been a marked rise in adult female literacy rates, which has been leading to converging male and female literacy rates. (However, surveys that probe more deeply into family labour market behaviour often find that many more women are in fact working outside the home than are usually reported.) As a consequence, the vast majority of men work in male-dominated occupations.

Many countries in the region are statist if not militarist and the authorities are unwilling to diversify, delegate and decentralize. They are, by and large, ill-prepared for an era of market liberalization. And many of them are in a state of readiness for armed conflict, which, of course, entails severe welfare costs and contributes to the usually large size of the government sector (and hence employment in that sector). Most countries have had a tradition of some government-provided support for the population at large, especially in the form of food subsidies. The oil-rich Gulf Cooperation Council countries until recently guaranteed well-paid, public-sector employment to their nationals, although recent fiscal difficulties have ended that. Employment in public enterprises, however, has usually been protected, often effectively putting a brake on private-sector development.

*Africa*

Compared with West Asia, the countries of North Africa have been actively restructuring their economies, diversifying and preparing for greater trade liberalization as well as allowing greater scope for private business activity. In Morocco, this appears to have led to some growth in real wages. Little, however, is known about changes in poverty levels. In Egypt, in the first half of the 1990s, it is estimated that real per capita expenditure fell in the cities by 3 per cent and in the countryside by 10 per cent. Average income per income receiver apparently fell considerably more than this, suggesting that more household members had to work, at a lower average wage, in order to sustain per capita consumption. Nonetheless, the distribution of income has apparently not worsened (the same applies to Morocco). ILO data bear out a fall in real wages in manufacturing in Egypt in recent years.

In Egypt the open unemployment rate has been steadily rising since the late 1970s and was estimated at 11 per cent in 1995 (with the rate for women double that of men).[14] Elsewhere, rates are reported as 18 per cent in Morocco (23 per cent for women, 16 per cent for men), 15 per cent in Tunisia, 16 per cent in North Sudan; 26 per cent in Algeria (similar for men and women). In Mauritania, urban unemployment is estimated at 25–30 per cent. This is a particularly serious problem, since Mauritania's population, which used to be largely nomadic, is now almost 50 per cent urban.

As in West Asia, the labour force situation of women differs from that of men. In Morocco, for example, female labour force participation rates are some 33 per cent of the rate for men in urban areas, but only 18 per cent of the male rate in rural areas. Highly educated women, however, do figure strongly in the labour force and nearly one-third of urban scientific and professional workers are women. It is the less educated women who have fewer opportunities.

The features of the Maghreb countries just described are not typical of Africa as a whole. Of course, the African continent demonstrates considerable heterogeneity, so generalizations concerning developments in a large number of individual countries would be unwise. The general picture has been one of fluctuating economic growth rates from a low base and of a relatively high rate of population growth, from which high levels of poverty are likely to follow. Thus, for example, for 17 sub-Saharan African countries for which the ILO has recent data on the share of the population living on less than one US dollar per day (at constant 1985 prices), the median figure is about 45 per cent. For North Africa, the score is about 2 to 4 per cent.[15] What wage data there are show generally falling wage levels, and stagnation in South Africa, where paid employment has also been falling. Such indicators of poverty imply a particularly difficult time for women, who often have to supplement the family income in poor-quality jobs, not least in order to earn the money to pay for their children's education, for

which the State no longer properly provides. Women's labour force participation has risen, for example, by 7 percentage points in urban Kenya over
10 years. Of course, the continent has its bright spots – Botswana and
Uganda are often cited, not to mention Mauritius – and there has been
growth in francophone West Africa following the CFA franc devaluation of
1994. Indeed, out of 48 sub-Saharan African countries, 37 recorded positive economic growth for the period 1994–97.[16] But experience suggests
that growth is rarely sustained and it is certainly insufficient to shift the
economic structure towards greater industrialization and job stability. Most
countries show a very high share of the labour force in agriculture – in the
70–80 per cent range; some even show a fall in the share of the labour force
in industry. However, urbanization is far advanced in a number of countries, including Kenya, South Africa and Zimbabwe.

Since the mid-1990s the informal sector in urban Africa has continued
to grow, with women predominating in the lowest productivity activities,
just as they do in most of peasant agriculture. But the dichotomy between
formal and informal activities is increasingly unable to do justice to the
heterogeneity of employment relationships. Regular wage employment in
large enterprises has fallen, a process that began in the late 1980s. Public-
enterprise employment has fallen, often with privatization, but public
administration has sometimes been slow to cut its numbers. Unemployment is often very high but remains an urban phenomenon. Urban
unemployment is reportedly as high as 33 per cent in Mauritania (de Luca,
op. cit.), but occasional household surveys report that the rate is generally
in the 10–25 per cent range, including 17 per cent in Lagos in 1995 and
some 25 per cent in South Africa (ILO, KILM).[17] In a few countries, open
unemployment has been falling in recent years, either because jobseekers
are going directly into the informal sector (where at least two-thirds will,
anyway, find work) or because of spasmodic upturns in economic activity.

As in many other regions that have been following a path of deregulation over the past few years, the use of temporary work contracts in larger
enterprises, earlier very rare, appears to be spreading quickly.[18] In
Mauritania and Mali, the ratio of temporary to permanent workers is 2:3,
in Senegal 1:4 and in Benin 1:2. Temporary workers are paid much less
and, of course, are in a far more precarious position as regards job security than other workers in the enterprise. The growing use of temporary
workers has led to lower urban incomes and to the narrowing of the
rural–urban income gap. Meanwhile, the informal sector, largely defined as
enterprises employing five people or fewer, which has been providing an
increasing share of urban incomes, has become more service-oriented, with
greater female participation rates. The share of small-scale enterprises

employing wage earners is small and often falling (from 18 per cent of small-scale sector employment to, respectively, 13 per cent in Burkina Faso and 10 per cent in Mali in the years before 1995). Thus the fall in wage employment in Africa is not confined to the larger enterprises. The informal sector is obviously playing a necessary role in absorbing workers, but its capacity to improve working conditions, let alone to invest and expand, is very weak.

A basic employment problem in many African countries is low productivity in agriculture, which persists despite the efforts of structural adjustment programmes to make imported food relatively expensive and the expanded cultivation of domestic substitutes more profitable. No doubt this has occurred to some extent, but the capacity of local producers to take advantage of price incentives is limited for a number of reasons, including: low land fertility, as population growth pushes cultivation on to lower-quality soils; poor transport and roads, as the budget for road maintenance is negligible; expensive inputs; and lack of extension services. Many African cultivators are women, which can be an additional obstacle to their receiving help to upgrade their farming methods.

## Latin America and the Caribbean[19]

At the end of the twentieth century, Latin America and the Caribbean were overwhelmingly urban; very few of the countries in the region had a majority of their population in rural areas and, for the region as a whole, close to 80 per cent of the workforce was urban. In addition, most workers in a majority of the countries were employees, not self-employed. Earlier trends in the sectoral composition of employment extended into the 1990s, and goods-producing sectors continued to lose their employment share, especially in agriculture and manufacturing. By 1997, average labour productivity in agriculture in the region was almost equal to that of services, the former rising, the latter falling; meanwhile, labour productivity in industry grew very rapidly, widening the gap between it and the average for the economy.

Probably since 1995, unemployment has risen in most countries of the region, 1999 being a particularly bad year, bringing a large rise in unemployment in Argentina, Chile, Colombia, Uruguay and Venezuela, as table 2.5 shows. Mexico, however, is an outstanding exception. The data all refer to urban areas only and have been collected using the same methodology.

Female participation rates have continued to rise significantly; between 1980 and 1995 the rate (defined as the labour force of all ages divided by the population aged 15–64) rose from 35 per cent to 44.5 per cent as the

**Table 2.5**   Latin America and the Caribbean: Urban unemployment rate, 1970–99 (as a percentage)

| Country | 1970 | 1995 | 1996 | 1997 | 1998 | 1999[1] |
|---|---|---|---|---|---|---|
| Argentina | 4.9 | 17.5 | 17.3 | 14.9 | 12.9 | 15.5[2] |
| Brazil | 3.7 | 4.6 | 5.4 | 5.7 | 7.6 | 7.7 |
| Chile | 3.9 | 6.6 | 5.4 | 5.3 | 6.4 | 9.8[2] |
| Colombia | 10.0 | 8.8 | 11.2 | 12.4 | 15.2 | 19.8 |
| Costa Rica | 3.5 | 5.7 | 6.6 | 5.9 | 5.4 | n.a. |
| El Salvador | n.a. | 7.0 | 5.8 | 7.5 | 7.6 | 8.0 |
| Honduras | n.a. | 6.6 | 6.6 | 5.2 | 5.8 | 5.4 |
| Mexico | 7.2 | 6.2 | 5.5 | 3.7 | 3.2 | 2.6 |
| Panama | 10.3 | 16.4 | 16.9 | 15.4 | 15.5 | 13.0 |
| Peru | 8.3 | 7.9 | 7.9 | 8.4 | 8.2 | 9.8 |
| Uruguay | 7.5 | 10.8 | 12.3 | 11.6 | 10.2 | 12.1 |
| Venezuela | 7.8 | 10.3 | 11.8 | 11.4 | 11.3 | 15.3 |

n.a. = figures not available.
Notes:   [1]Second quarter figures. [2]Figures for 1999.
Sources:   ILO: *Yearbook of Labour Statistics* (Geneva, various years); *Informa: Panorama laboral* (Lima, various years).

share of women in the total labour force rose from 27 per cent to 33 per cent. (The corresponding male participation rate moved down very slightly.) Female rates tend to be positively associated with education, with single status (especially if household head) and, for those who are married, with a small family. Participation has tended to increase over time for women in each family status and educational category. Rates for married women appear to have been rising particularly sharply, all apparently reflecting a process of generally improving social change.

A recent phenomenon in the region is that, as unemployment rates have risen, its incidence has tended to be highest in the lowest income quintile of urban families; except for Mexico with its very low overall rates, the figure ranges from 17 per cent in Brazil to over 40 per cent in Venezuela, dropping usually to 1–3 per cent in the top quintile.[20] In the 1970s, unemployment rates were often lower and more similar for all groups. This corroborates the increasing concern over the unemployment of less educated workers. In addition, older workers are increasingly subject to open unemployment in periods of recession.

As elsewhere, there is a growing trend towards temporary and part-time work, although the precise magnitude of the phenomenon is not clear. It is widely believed that the earlier rapid growth of temporary work was partly a response to rigid job security legislation, which made it hard to dismiss permanent workers. Legislative changes of the early 1990s presumably facilitated some of this increase but much had already occurred de facto. In practice, there has been a widespread tendency for labour legislation to be ignored or bypassed, which has resulted in an increasing proportion of people working in the region with no formal contract or legislated protection. This is particularly noticeable in Argentina and Brazil.

For decades, Latin America has suffered a rise in income inequality that has often been most acute during recessions and economic reforms. Where reform coincided with recession, recovery typically did not bring the inequality back to its pre-recession level. The main approach to explaining inequality has emphasized the wide gap between the wages of skilled and less skilled (or educated) workers. But while real wages have, since 1995, tended to creep up from their 1991 low, this has come with a substantial increase in the gap between white- and blue-collar workers, most notably in Peru (by more than 30 per cent), Colombia and Mexico. Often, this also coincides with an increasing gender wage gap.

The size of the informal sector in Latin America is often taken as a measure of the failure of the region's economy to generate reasonably remunerative jobs, although as its share rises the sector is no doubt becoming more heterogeneous. ILO figures show the informal sector's share of employment rising from 52 per cent in 1990 to 57 per cent in 1996, implying that it has accounted for the majority of net new jobs. In almost all the region's countries, paid employment grew fastest in small and very small enterprises, which, by the definition adopted by the region, are part of the informal sector and no doubt where labour conditions in general are most in need of upgrading and protection. The economic crisis of the 1980s tended to expand the size of the informal sector rather than raise unemployment rates. This trade-off may now have disappeared, since both unemployment and the informal sector have been rising in Argentina, Brazil, Peru and Venezuela. And, as previously noted, unemployment rates are generally highest for the poor, that is, those people who usually draw their incomes from the informal sector. This again adds to the unequal distribution of income found throughout the region.

The Caribbean countries present a diverse picture, although unemployment is usually in double digits (despite a tendency for it to fall in recent years). Emphasis in these countries has been placed far less on, for example, the behaviour of the informal sector and more on choosing the most appropriate macroeconomic policy framework to suit their very open economic structure. Some countries, such as Jamaica and Haiti, are facing considerable inflation and are attempting to tackle it partly by setting a fixed nominal exchange rate. But this has been associated with an appreciated real exchange rate and negligible employment and output growth. By contrast, the Dominican Republic has had strong export and output growth and a falling real exchange rate, combined with low rates of price inflation.

The country's strong export growth has, however, been linked with poor labour conditions. The macroeconomic situation in Trinidad and Tobago is fairly similar. In Barbados, output growth has been falling and consumer prices are near stable, helped by an exchange rate anchor and a negotiated approach to wage and price determination. A fall in unemployment in a context of low output growth, as seems to have occurred in Jamaica, usually indicates a shift to a greater share of informal activities and lower wages.

### Western Europe, North America and Australasia

A major feature of the labour market in Western Europe at the end of the 1990s was the failure of a number of countries to create any new jobs, at a time of high unemployment (see table 2.6). This applied particularly to the larger continental European countries; there was significant employment growth in many of the smaller countries. Indeed, the rise was particularly large in Ireland, the Netherlands and Norway. Although some of these rises were more the result of a rebound after a period of job losses, others, such as in Ireland and the Netherlands, were not. The poor results in France and Italy since 1995 are a continuation of past trends.[21] Country behaviour is thus increasingly divergent, casting doubt on the existence of any single "European model" to set against a "United States model".

Table 2.6 shows employment growth and labour demand for the following groups of countries: the United States and Canada (North America); Australia and New Zealand; four of the larger European continental countries (France, Germany, Italy and Spain); the United Kingdom (shown separately as representing an alternative approach to labour market regulation); and the rest of the EU. The second line for each group or country (ii) shows employment growth deflated by population growth on the argument that a part of employment growth is not necessarily policy related but reflects a rising population. There is some justification for this argument and, compared with North America, it presents the experience of the smaller EU countries favourably. However, as it can be said that good job-creation policies pull in more migrants, the series for population growth should, arguably, refer only to natural population growth and exclude migration. A complication here is that, although migration into North America has been higher than into Europe, the effect of migration on the population growth of Europe has been greater. Consequently, the differences in employment growth and population deflated employment growth between North America and the small EU countries would be little affected by migration. The final line in the table for each group or country

**Table 2.6** Industrialized countries: Employment growth and labour demand, 1993–99 (1992=100)

| Country | 1993 | 1994 | 1995 | 1996 | 1997 | 1998 | 1999 |
|---|---|---|---|---|---|---|---|
| *North America* | | | | | | | |
| (i) Employment growth | 101.0 | 103.6 | 105.0 | 106.6 | 108.7 | 110.5 | 112.3 |
| (ii) Deflated by population growth | 100.0 | 101.6 | 102.0 | 102.4 | 103.4 | 103.9 | 104.4 |
| (iii) x index of hours worked | 101.0 | 102.9 | 103.0 | 102.4 | 104.4 | 103.3 | n.a. |
| | | | | | | | |
| *Australia/New Zealand* | | | | | | | |
| (i) Employment growth | 101.0 | 103.8 | 108.0 | 109.5 | 110.4 | 112.4 | 114.5 |
| (ii) Deflated by population growth | 99.6 | 101.8 | 104.0 | 104.0 | 103.5 | 104.1 | 104.8 |
| | | | | | | | |
| (Australia only) | | | | | | | |
| (iii) x index of hours worked | 101.0 | 103.5 | 106.0 | 104.9 | 104.2 | 103.8 | n.a. |
| | | | | | | | |
| *France, Germany, Italy and Spain* | | | | | | | |
| (i) Employment growth | 97.7 | 97.0 | 97.4 | 97.8 | 97.8 | 98.6 | 100.1 |
| (ii) Deflated by population growth | 97.6 | 96.5 | 96.7 | 96.8 | 96.6 | 97.2 | 98.3 |
| (iii) x index of hours worked | 97.5 | 96.3 | 95.9 | 95.6 | 95.5 | 97.5 | n.a. |
| | | | | | | | |
| *United Kingdom* | | | | | | | |
| (i) Employment growth | 98.8 | 99.6 | 101.0 | 101.6 | 103.3 | 104.2 | 105.2 |
| (ii) Deflated by population growth | 98.1 | 99.1 | 99.7 | 102.2 | 102.4 | 102.9 | 103.5 |
| (iii) x index of hours worked | 99.3 | 100.2 | 102.0 | 101.6 | 103.2 | 102.6 | n.a. |
| | | | | | | | |
| *EU–15* (minus the five listed above) | | | | | | | |
| (i) Employment growth | 98.8 | 99.5 | 101.0 | 101.9 | 103.2 | 105.6 | 107.9 |
| (ii) Deflated by population growth | 98.1 | 98.6 | 99.7 | 100.4 | 101.5 | 103.6 | 105.6 |
| (iii) x index of hours worked | 97.0 | 100.1 | 100.0 | 103.0 | 102.0 | n.a. | n.a. |

n.a. = not available.
Notes: (i) Employment growth equals numbers of civilian employment; (ii) deflated by population growth equals the growth of civilian employment divided by the growth of population (also 1992 = 100); (iii) the final line is population-deflated employment growth multiplied by an index of hours worked, taken from national sources.
Sources: OECD: *Employment Outlook* (Paris, various years); Eurostat: *Labour Force Survey results* (Luxembourg, various years).

(iii) includes an index of hours worked, which generally appears to move procyclically.

These data on employment growth hide some massive shifts in the workforce. The share of employed men aged 25–54 fell over the longer period 1985–97 by 12 percentage points in Spain and Sweden and by 5–7 percentage points in Austria, France, Germany and Italy. (And it should be noted that the employment rate for low-skilled men is usually only about 85 per cent of the average.) Employment rates for men in the 55–64 age bracket fell in many countries by a good 10 percentage points. For women aged 25–54, rates rose by 4–7 percentage points in Germany, France and Italy, and by a massive 23 percentage points in Ireland, 18 in the Netherlands, 13 in Spain and ten in the United Kingdom.

Since 1995, unemployment rates have remained extremely high in Spain (although they fell from 24 per cent in 1994 to 16 per cent in 1999) and are bunched around 11 per cent in Belgium, Finland, France and Italy. Elsewhere, figures have converged to about 5–7 per cent, although Germany, at around 9 per cent, sits between the two groups. But high rates in a number of large countries are keeping the European average up. That men have become less likely to be employed does not mean that they became unemployed; many are no longer in the labour force. Nor is the fact that the greater number of women seeking jobs is responsible for high rates of unemployment. As the ILO's *World Employment Report 1998–99* points out, in the European countries where unemployment increased, the activity rate (employed plus unemployed as a share of total population) hardly rose over a long period.

The large number of people who stay unemployed for long periods of time is a matter of such growing concern that the European Commission has made the issue the subject of one of its employment guidelines (that is, retraining for those out of work for 12 months or more). The rate of long-term (12 months plus) unemployment to the total labour force ranged, in 1997, from over 11 per cent in Spain to below 1 per cent in Norway. Generally, it was in the 2.5–5 per cent range. Only in the countries with relatively fast employment growth have rates of long-term employment fallen, and rates have risen in countries with sluggish employment growth. The level of long-term unemployment and its behaviour partly reflect the different country use of labour market programmes, which have the effect of substituting short periods of unemployment (perhaps for more people) for longer periods.

In contrast to Europe, both the United States and Canada (and Australia), despite many differences in labour market policy, have seen rates of employment growth rise faster than that of the labour force, although unemployment remains somewhat higher in Canada (and in Australia) than in the United States, where unemployment in 1999 was down from a high of 6.9 per cent in 1993 to 4.2 per cent. Furthermore, the US employment rate for men is higher than that of any EU country except Denmark and for women higher than any except Denmark and Sweden. All this is *a priori* evidence that the United States is closer to full employment than many European countries, although the pick-up in labour demand in several of the latter has recently been very strong.[22] The *World Employment Report 1998–99* explains how the US economy has been creating both relatively well-paid and relatively low-paid jobs (and few jobs in the middle-income category), which implies that the distribution of wages must, by some measure, have become more unequal. The country's wage inequality, however, is largely related to relative education and training levels and not to any growing division by gender or ethnic group. Indeed, these divisions have narrowed. The real average wage for production workers, which is around the median for all workers, was nonetheless stagnant for a long time (and only in 1997 regained its 1989 level). And, because of the high level of employment growth, combined with sustained but not always spectacular output growth, labour productivity growth was low until a number of parameters apparently began to change after 1998. The so-called "new economy" of the United States is discussed in Chapter 3.

Table 2.7 sheds more light on wage behaviour in the United States and contrasts it with that in France for the two periods 1986–90 and 1990–97. The first row gives the figure for average wages in the economy (compensation of employees per wage earner). "Ordinary" workers' wages (second row) grew faster than the average in France and slower than the average in the United States. (In the United States they grew by 2.4 per cent in 1998, compared with only 0.4 per cent annually over a seven-year period.) The last three rows show output growth subdivided into employment growth and labour productivity (GDP per worker). It can be noted that workers' wages in France, while rising faster than the average, nonetheless rose below the rate of productivity growth. Average wages in France rose substantially less than productivity growth. In the United States, as average wages grew between the two periods their distance from productivity growth narrowed substantially.

Much of the increase in employment in Europe in recent years has been in part-time work; in 1997 nearly 18 per cent of all EU employees were working part time of which nearly one-quarter of them would have preferred full-time work. Over 80 per cent of part-time workers are women, (Temporary, whether full- or part-time, work accounted for about 12 per cent of employment, of which some 40 per cent was involuntary.) In many countries, in both North America and Western Europe, when total employment grew, average hours also grew, and vice versa, reinforcing the cyclical nature of employment growth (see table 2.6). But this finding is too crude to determine whether there is a trade-off between hours and jobs and thus scope to reduce hours by legislation and thereby raise employment. In the post-1995 period, some countries, such as Denmark, attempted to limit hours worked either by discouraging overtime or by moving to a shorter working week (as France is currently doing). In Norway, hours worked have also fallen sharply. However, it is a fallacy to think that work can simply be divided up among a variable number of workers. Naturally, there is likely to be a general preference in society for a shorter working week, provided that it can be achieved without weakening employment and output

**Table 2.7**    France and the United States: Annual wage growth in real terms, 1986–90 and 1990–97

| | France | | United States | | |
|---|---|---|---|---|---|
| | 1986–90 | 1990–97 | 1986–90 | 1990–97 | (1997–98) |
| Compensation of employees per wage earner (average wage) | 0.2 | 0.5 | 0.1 | 1.0 | |
| Workers' wage[1] | 1.0 | 0.7 | -1.3 | 0.4 | (2.4) |
| Output growth | 3.2 | 1.3 | 2.7 | 2.6 | |
| Employment growth | 1.8 | 0.2 | 2.1 | 1.3 | |
| GDP per worker | 1.4 | 1.1 | 0.6 | 1.3 | |

Note:    [1]In France, hourly earnings of non-agricultural workers (*ouvriers*); in the United States, production workers in the private sector.

Sources:  OECD: *Main Economic Indicators* (Paris, various years); *Annuaire Statistique de la France* (Paris, various years); US Department of Labor, Employment and Earnings (various years).

growth. Nonetheless, some involuntary part-time work is probably inevitable. To the extent that faster growth removes this involuntary part of part-time work, the resulting increase in hours worked should also be welcomed.

If those countries in Western Europe that have been unable to create new jobs are to absorb the unemployed, they will have to deal with two particular problems reasonably promptly: they will need to secure a faster and sustained rate of overall output growth on the one hand, and come to terms with, very probably, a lower rate of labour productivity growth, on the other. In principle, employment, output and labour productivity are determined simultaneously, but in fact there is some scope for policies to trade off productivity against employment. In some major continental countries, if a high rate of labour productivity growth (say 3 per cent annually) continues, then absorbing the unemployed over a period of ten years (and making an allowance for those who would subsequently wish to join or rejoin the labour force) could give a necessary GDP growth rate of around 5 per cent or more. Conversely, an output growth rate of a more likely 2.5 per cent annually would suggest that productivity growth over, say, a ten-year period, in which full employment was achieved could hardly exceed 1 per cent, which is even lower than the figure for the United States before its recent upturn in productivity.

The simplest way to achieve lower productivity growth (which the Netherlands has done) is to expand the share of low-productivity activities in the total by deregulating labour markets and encouraging part-time work. But without countervailing and consensual policies, this is likely to lead to increased wage dispersion. One way of sidestepping this problem, which has been taken to great lengths in France, is by subsidizing employment. In France, this now accounts for 10 per cent of total employment (and up to 25 per cent for the 16–24 age group). However, this is costly and can in the long term be demoralizing, not least because it presents no opportunities for individual advancement. In the medium to long run the answer no doubt lies in upgrading skills so that the low-educated sections of the labour force virtually disappear. But the solution of expanding serv- ices by, for example, deregulating hours of work and opening times (which is often favoured by the European Commission) is not practical, particu- larly if it increases wage inequality and segmentation in the labour market to a socially unacceptable degree.

The United States has a different set of problems to cope with. Until recently, wage stagnation among production workers was the norm, even at fairly high levels of output growth. This drew more workers into the labour force, often those with relatively low skills, in order to sustain household incomes; the challenge for training policy is thus immense. Higher levels of productivity are being achieved on average but higher productivity for all workers would be desirable, which requires both more training and investment.

## 2.3 Broad issues of employment quality

*Introduction*

As has already been mentioned, certain aspects of employment quality are virtually impossible to measure; only anecdotal evidence of their suitabili- ty and degree of change is available, which is unacceptable for analysis. Information on the extent of respect for health and safety provisions and the level of protection they give unfortunately falls into this category. So, to a large extent, does the coverage and development of training, where only changes in some correlates can be observed.[23]

Change in income security is another aspect of employment quality that cannot easily be measured. Income security for most workers comprises three elements: stable business conditions, security of job tenure and mech- anisms for income compensation. Many farmers and self-employed people, especially those in the informal sector, have no security of tenure, only different conditions governing their use of and control over income- generating assets. And their only means of compensation for lost income is to draw on their own savings or to try to diversify the sources of family income.

In many countries there is now greater scope for a more sophisticated approach to systems of income compensation. Many developing countries have long had systems of compulsory savings for workers, albeit usually not for those in very small enterprises. However, the intention of schemes of the provident-fund type is to provide people with an alternative to a retirement pension, rather than income support in the event of unemployment. If they are drawn on prematurely, they are no longer effective as a source of retirement income. Introducing unemployment insurance only becomes feasible when the likelihood of unemployment is, in normal times, quite low. That was precisely the situation in many East Asian countries before the late 1997 Asian financial crisis; long-term worker commitment to the enterprise was strong and unemployment low. The corollary, of course, is that, for these very same reasons, many workers saw little need to contribute to such schemes, since they believed the likelihood of their becoming unemployed was extremely low.

The Asian crisis came after a decade or two in which the sources of income in many East Asian workers' households had become less diversified, and this greater specialization had gone hand in hand with higher incomes. To that extent, the need for income compensation systems had been gradually increasing, although it had gone largely unnoticed. Asian workers were, however, considered fortunate to have had that opportunity. Many workers throughout the world are finding themselves in an increasingly loose relationship with a final employing enterprise (see the regional sections of this chapter). Some are effectively subcontracted as a means of spreading the enterprise workload or avoiding contractual obligations. Others, even in wealthier countries, have a relationship no different from casual labourers looking for a day's work.

Developments in two other aspects of employment quality are discussed next: freedom of association; and the promotion of women in the labour force, discrimination and equality of opportunity.[24]

## *Freedom of association*

In some countries extreme situations still exist where independent workers' organizations are totally prohibited, under a penalty of imprisonment or, for migrants, expulsion.[25] However, more often, labour legislation draws distinctions between, and excludes from its scope, specific groups of workers; for those workers who are subsequently not able to establish organizations within the purview of the law, this situation is tantamount to a ban. Such exclusion is all the more disturbing where it relates to workers coming from the poorest and most underprivileged segments of the population. Limitations on the establishment of organizations may also stem from conditions relating to nationality, sex, opinion or political affiliation.

Restrictions based on nationality can seriously limit migrant workers from playing an active role in the defence of their interests, especially in sectors where they are the main source of labour.

In other countries, the right to organize is not contested but restrictions prevent workers and employers from establishing organizations of their own choosing. These restrictions can range from containment, where organizations operate only within a limited environment and cannot freely organize further, to the prohibition of legitimate means by which organizations exert pressure to further their members' interests, such as the right to strike.

A number of countries impose rules on the establishment of workers' organizations that are related, among other things, to the formalities to be observed when an organization is created or to issues of membership, recognition or the representativeness of the organizations. Although the right to establish organizations does not imply absolute freedom, requirements are sometimes so stringent or complex that they amount to forbidding workers or employers from organizing freely or to giving the authorities discretionary power to refuse the establishment of such organizations.[26] Related to this are requirements that only one trade union can be established for a given category of workers. Union monopoly is still explicitly provided for in a number of countries, including in some parts of North Africa and the Middle East, but progress has been achieved elsewhere, most notably in Central and Eastern Europe and in Africa, where many countries had earlier banned trade union pluralism.

Except in extremely rare cases, relating, for instance, to public or essential services, international labour Conventions stipulate that the right to strike is a legitimate means of action for workers' organizations to further the interests of their members. However, there are countries in all regions that put restrictions on strikes in general; some of these refer essentially to the maintenance of essential services, although in some instances such services are widely interpreted to include, for example, metropolitan transport, postal services or even department stores and pleasure parks. Many countries also reserve a right to compulsory arbitration before or during a strike, after which any strike is considered illegal.

Finally, the exercise of freedom of association implies that all individuals involved in trade union activities shall enjoy adequate protection against acts of anti-union discrimination. However, the extent to which the authorities provide protection against these acts varies widely; acts of victimization against those attempting to organize workers are reported by countries at all income levels.

*The promotion of women in the labour force, discrimination and equality of opportunity*

The share of women in the global labour force is rising and, by generally acceptable estimates, is currently some 35–40 per cent of total employment. Women's education levels are generally lower than those of men but are catching up. Their activity rates have often risen sharply over the past decade, while those of men have usually been falling slightly. As workers, women and men have a wide range of identical concerns, but their circumstances and often their position in the labour force can differ widely; many labour market policies need to include an explicit recognition of this gender dimension. Firstly, occupational segregation by sex is found worldwide and takes two forms: horizontal segregation, that is, the distribution of men and women across occupations (for example, women working as maids, men as truck drivers); and vertical segregation, where men and women work in the same occupation but one sex is more likely to be at a higher grade (for example, women as production workers, men as production supervisors). Approximately one-half of both male and female workers are in "gender-dominated" occupations, where at least 80 per cent of the workers are of the same sex. However, male-dominated, non-agricultural occupations are over seven times as numerous as female-dominated occupations. Among professional and technical occupations, women often work as nurses and teachers; they also dominate in clerical and secretarial jobs and in many service occupations. "Female" occupations tend to be considered less valuable, with generally lower pay, lower status and fewer advancement possibilities.[27] Women workers are much more likely than men to face competition at work from the other sex. They are also more likely to be employed in smaller rather than large enterprises and, by extension, in the informal sector.

The levels of occupational segregation by sex differ greatly across regions. Asia has the lowest average level and the Middle East and North Africa the highest. The level of sex segregation is relatively high in other developing regions, while OECD member countries and Central and Eastern Europe display average levels. In Asia, the gender dimension seems to have a somewhat different character, and vertical segregation within occupations is more significant than elsewhere. But women in Asia, and in other developing countries that have followed export-oriented industrial paths, are more likely to be production workers than women in developing countries in general. To that extent, occupational segregation worldwide is not related to socio-economic development, and differences between countries are largely region specific. This strongly implies that social, cultural and historical factors are of paramount importance in determining the extent to which occupations are segmented in relation to the sex of the worker.

In the past two decades occupational segregation by sex has fallen slightly, owing more to the increased integration of men and women within occupations than to any shift in the occupational structure of employment. Frequently, the rate of expansion of established female-dominated occupations has been insufficient to absorb all new female labour force participants, and so many women have entered less traditional occupations.[28] However, this has not occurred in the larger East Asian countries and in most Middle Eastern and North African countries. Occupational segregation by sex has increased in China and remained unchanged in Japan.

Within the past few years there has been a marked increase in the adoption of national laws and legal practices requiring the payment of equal remuneration between men and women for work of equal value (in conformity with the ILO's Equal Remuneration Convention, 1951 (No. 100)). The concept of work of equal value as the point of comparison between jobs is intended to reach the partly concealed discrimination that may arise from the existence of different occupational categories for men and women.

Despite government efforts to eliminate discrimination and promote equal opportunity and treatment, practices resulting in the social exclusion, marginalization and even persecution of particular groups of people, both women and men, continue to be widespread. Most countries have adopted legal provisions to protect against discrimination on at least some of the grounds listed in Chapter 1. Many have gone further, adopting guarantees of equal opportunity and treatment and establishing enforcement mechanisms, particularly for workers with a clear employment relationship in enterprises above a certain size. Given the insidious nature of some forms of discrimination and the difficulty in detecting and remedying discrimination, let alone the problem of equating the value of work in sex-segregated occupations, the use of corrective mechanisms is seen as a positive indicator of progress in combating discrimination. Correspondingly, the lack of knowledge of the issue and the absence of complaints or corrective mechanisms are probably signs that discrimination in a country is going unchecked. Discrimination in employment makes little theoretical sense in that it may well prevent the best equipped people from doing a job. However, K. J. Arrow points out that explanations of discrimination based on the logic of profit and loss cannot account for the role it seems to play in everyday behaviour.[29]

Women suffer from multiple forms of discrimination if they are a part of a racial, ethnic or religious minority or an indigenous community. The ILO Committee of Experts on the Application of Conventions and Recommendations has remarked that discrimination linked to religion is the most sensitive aspect of discrimination practised against women. In addition, difficulties deriving from disability, marital status or age are often compounded by gender-based discrimination.

In recent years, concerns over discrimination on the grounds of political opinion have waned with the general dissolution of communist-controlled regimes and the move towards democracy in many countries. But other forms of discrimination based on race, national extraction or ethnic origin appear to be on the rise. Discrimination can also take the form of preventing or severely discouraging internal, domestic labour mobility and thus preventing, for example, villagers from applying for jobs in towns. While not all minority groups suffer from discriminatory treatment, some are singled out and even become targets. These forms of discrimination are often so culturally driven and intractable that if left unresolved they can lead to war. The growing concern over continuing acts of racial intolerance and hatred can be seen by the large number of new laws being established to punish them. However, there are usually no clear lines as to what constitutes discrimination on grounds of race, national extraction, belonging to a minority group or colour, and these concepts often merge. They may be based on how the people concerned consider their differences and the attitudes that then result. Discrimination based on racial and national extraction may also include distinctions based on clan, tribe, or any groups of peoples, or populations defined by similar distinct characteristics such as language or cultural tradition. The Roma in Central and Eastern European countries are an example of a group that is often subject to discrimination in all aspects of their social and economic life. Discrimination against indigenous and tribal peoples has been of such an extreme and distinct nature that the ILO has adopted a specific Convention – the Indigenous and Tribal Peoples Convention, 1989 (No. 169) – with the aim of recognizing and protecting their self-determination and identity. Forms of discrimination based on the caste system, especially where low-caste status and poor-quality occupation go together, are essentially similar.

New forms of discrimination have recently emerged. In industrialized countries, where ageing populations are confronting slow growing levels of employment, not only may employers show a preference for younger workers and ease older workers out of jobs, they may also be encouraged by government policy to do so. And in some developing countries, people affected with HIV/AIDS are also facing discrimination on a daily basis.

As noted earlier, migrant workers can face discrimination in employment and jobseeking. The ILO has estimated that, in 1995, between 80 and 97 million people were residing, legally or illegally, in a country other than their own. Since this figure includes both migrant workers and their families, this means that probably between 2 and 3 per cent of the world's labour force are migrants.[30] Where migrant workers are accepted for permanent settlement, their locally born children may or may not be or become citizens of their country of residence. Even where they are citizens, they can face discrimination. In many Western European countries, roughly one in three job applicants of migrant origin has been found to be excluded from application procedures on discriminatory grounds.

A great deal of international migration is illegal (perhaps one-third of the total, or maybe nearly 1 per cent of the world's labour force). In good times, some countries with a perceived labour shortage in some market segments turn a blind eye to illegal migration, but reverse their attitude later. In many countries, legislation provides for sanctions against employers who hire undocumented workers, but enforcement varies greatly. Attempts have also been made to establish some control through amnesties, but these have often proved difficult to implement. Many undocumented migrants in fact entered the host country legally but overstayed their visa or violated its terms – usually by working. Furthermore, jobs given to illegal migrants offer almost certainly poor conditions so far as pay, health and safety, the remittance of earnings and most aspects of working relations are concerned. Clandestine jobseekers still feel that work under such conditions is acceptable, though, and some employers find it profitable to employ them.

The 1990s saw no relaxation in the rising demand for unskilled female migrant workers to take up housekeeping tasks, work as low-wage workers in labour-intensive industries, or in socially undesirable jobs, including the sex industry. Migration by young women workers has been increasing in recent years, most notably from South-East Asia to Central and Eastern Europe, where they are employed in occupations and sectors vulnerable to abuse and exploitation.

Much migration, to the industrialized countries in particular, is of the highly educated, many of whom are migrating from a number of poorer countries. Migration now adds 0.3–0.4 per cent annually to the US population[31] (providing, it is believed, about one-quarter of the bosses of Silicon Valley companies) and about 0.2 per cent annually to the population of the EU.[32] It is possible that labour market deregulation encouraging long hours of work and a lack of reliance on certified vocational training in recruitment are features of labour markets that are attracting more educated migrants.

## 2.4   Concluding remarks

Chapters 1 and 2 have argued that little significance can be attached to general statements about the world employment situation, largely because of the tremendous economic disparities between countries at different levels of development. What is growing income or job insecurity in one region may be commonplace in another. Nevertheless, there are instances when the reversal of social and economic gains is evident, as in the wake of the Asian financial crisis, when it could be said that the employment situation clearly worsened. Often, however, different indicators will point in different directions. Thus, Latin America has higher unemployment rates and greater income inequality than 10 years ago but is, nevertheless, displaying some real wage growth.

Economic disparities between countries are an important aspect in the assessment of the relative employment situation, but only up to a point. Economic growth alone does not dictate the pattern of employment development. Two further elements must be added: firstly, the notion of democratic processes, particularly freedom of association, the acceptance of the outcomes of collective bargaining, the absence of discrimination and greater equality of opportunity; and secondly, that of the distribution of wages and working conditions within a country. Thus, wealthier countries are not necessarily those with the best employment conditions, and fast economic growth need not entail an equally fast improvement in employment conditions. On the notion of democratic processes, specifically in relation to freedom of association, there is the difficulty of distinguishing between the adoption of legislation and its proper implementation. As already noted, workers who encourage trade union membership on the shop floor can face many practical obstacles, even when legislation is clearly supportive. And discrimination in employment remains widespread, although it is unlikely to be worsening. The relative employment position of women and certainly women's relative education level are improving. To that extent, equality of opportunity may be becoming a reality.

The introduction of a notion of income distribution or wage dispersion can be complex. At one level this can be seen as a formal–informal sector dichotomy, as noted in Chapter 1, but the definitions of those two sectors are far from being watertight. As the informal sector apparently grows, which it is doing in much of Latin America and Africa, so it is likely that it will become increasingly differentiated, particularly since (one of the few global trends that is reasonably definite) the education level of the labour force is generally rising. The dispersion of working conditions may, of course, follow the size distribution of enterprises and be better in the larger firms, but the distribution of earnings is likely to be determined by household-related and individual variables.

In looking at wage distribution, a further concern arises: the treatment of the unemployed. Are they to be seen as zero earners and as therefore further weighting the distribution of earnings towards inequality, irrespective of their consumption levels? Can unemployment be equated to low-income earning, and in whose eyes? As will be seen in Chapter 3 in a discussion of the experience of the "older" OECD member countries, some observers explicitly take this view and equally explicitly rate any employment, however low paid, as more desirable in welfare terms than unemployment status. This is, of course, an oversimplified approach and, as the chapter suggests, much depends on background factors. What is, however, generally accepted is that it is not because potential workers prefer to be unemployed that they are unemployed. Current levels of unemployment benefit do not discourage job acceptance (although job-search intensity is affected by the duration of unemployment benefit), but if they are linked to the loss of other benefits, they may do so. Clearly, both unemployment and low-paid employment should be viewed as negative features of employment and labour markets.

Are there then any general features of labour market development that can be seen as positive or negative in employment terms? Obviously, there are some black spots: many labour market developments in Central and Eastern Europe can be described as negative, despite the moves made towards democracy; and in sub-Saharan Africa, matters are scarcely improving. Many of these negative elements arise because of the way the market liberalization process is being managed and other programmes and policies neglected. The liberalization process itself is likely to generate additional job and income insecurity and to make certain industries unprofitable. In addition, it may promote traditionally low-skilled and low-paying industries. Thus, some countries in North Africa, for example, may be about to face a period of negative employment developments as they open up more to world markets. But this is not the end of the story, for governments retain the autonomy to follow anti-poverty and skills upgrading policies.

The employment effects of market liberalization (and thus of globalization) should certainly not be taken to be totally negative. For one thing, there have been widespread and beneficial political changes in many countries, not least because of increased international scrutiny. For another, the ability of industrialized countries to sustain fast growth over a long period, if assured, is a potent force for helping the rest of the world. The next chapter suggests how some regions can help themselves enjoy such benefits.

## Notes

[1] See the data given in M. Castells: *The rise of the network society* (Oxford, Blackwell Publishers, 1996).

[2] For data, see *ILO News, Latin America and the Caribbean* (1998); *Labour Overview* (Lima, 1998); and ILO–PREALC: *Mercado de trabajo en cifras, 1959–80* (Santiago, 1982). For a further discussion, see the section on Asia, below.

[3] All the following data are taken from the ILO's *Yearbook of Labour Statistics* (various years).

[4] This section draws on G. Renshaw: *Achieving full employment in the transition economies*, ILO Employment Paper 2000/7 (Geneva, 2000). Data are generally from the ECE. In this section, and in the corresponding section of Chapter 3, the discussion centres on the main employment problems as they present themselves in Central Europe, the Baltic States and the CIS, excluding the Central Asian States.

[5] See A. Nesporova: *Employment and labour market policies in transition economies* (Geneva, ILO, 1999).

[6] Using all economy data, nowhere else does a sustained fall in unit labour costs occur for as long a period as in Hungary (1990–98). More common has been a lengthy rise in unit labour costs (for example, in the Czech Republic between 1991–97, in Slovakia between 1991–96 and in Ukraine between 1993–96, after a large fall in 1992).

[7] This section updates the information provided to the Asian Regional Consultation on Follow-up to the World Summit for Social Development, Bangkok, 1999, in the report, *Towards full employment: Prospects and problems in Asia and the Pacific* (Bangkok, 1999). Additional data have been obtained from national sources and from the IMF: *International Financial Statistics* (various years).

[8] It reached 5.3 per cent in May 1999 and was at 4.3 per cent in May 2000. These results from the labour force survey are very seasonal.

[9] See T. Rawski: *China: Prospects for full employment*, ILO Employment and Training Paper, No. 45 (Geneva, 1999).

[10] Table 2.4 shows the urban unemployment rate at 6.4 per cent for 1998. This is an unofficial estimate, since the official rate is much lower (see table 2.1). The unofficial estimate assumes that "furloughed" workers are available for work but that only a minority found work. The estimates are from Angang (H. Angang: "High unemployment rates will be difficult to reverse", in *China Economic Times*, 13 October 1998, quoted in Rawski, op. cit.).

[11] See A. R. Khan: *Macro policies and poverty alleviation, China*, Paper presented at the Asian Regional Workshop on Macro Policies and Micro Interventions for Poverty Alleviation (Bangkok, ILO, 1997).

[12] See ILO: *World Employment Report 1998–99: Employability in the global economy, How training matters* (Geneva, 1998).

[13] See ILO: *Yearbook of Labour Statistics* (Geneva, various years).

[14] See L. de Luca: *Employment in North Africa*, mimeo. (Geneva, ILO, 1999).

[15] Data on headcount poverty are given in ILO: *Key Indicators of the Labour Market 1999* (Geneva, 1999).

[16] However, the larger countries in terms of population, such as Ethiopia, Kenya, Nigeria, South Africa and the Democratic Republic of the Congo, have not been showing sustained growth in recent years. Collier and Gunning also suggest that episodes of fast growth have been the result of policy reforms, but that subsequent levels of foreign aid and investment have not been high enough to keep

growth at that level. See P. Collier and J. W. Gunning: *The IMF's role in structural adjustment,* World Bank Working Paper WPS/99–18 (Washington, DC, 1999).

[17] See also ILO: *World Employment Report 1998–99,* op. cit. Unemployment data in sub-Saharan Africa are not regularly available. Some surveys are carried out, often for other purposes, and their findings on unemployment, where reported, are not necessarily consistent in terms of methodology.

[18] See N. Pages: *La promotion du plein emploi en Afrique de l'Ouest et Centrale,* mimeo. (Geneva, ILO, 1998).

[19] This section draws largely on A. Berry and M. T. Mendez: *Policies to promote adequate employment in Latin America and the Caribbean,* ILO Employment and Training Working Paper, No. 46 (Geneva, 1999). Employment data are taken from the ILO's annual *Panorama laboral,* published by the ILO's Regional Office for the Americas in Lima.

[20] The ILO's *Panorama laboral* for 1999 summarized the situation for all of Latin America in 1998 as unemployment rates in the poorest two quintiles being some 4.4 times that of the richest decile and rates for the intermediate group as 1.9 times that of the top decile.

[21] Some improvements were noted in 2000.

[22] See P. Auer: *Employment revival in Europe: Labour market success in Austria, Denmark, Ireland and the Netherlands* (Geneva, ILO, 2000).

[23] Thus training is known to be more common in larger enterprises than in smaller firms, so, to that extent, there may increasingly be less training at the enterprise level. However, within the OECD and some Latin American countries, government-sponsored training as a means of aiding the long-term and young unemployed to find work is known to be increasing.

[24] Information on these areas is available from the reports of the ILO's Committee of Experts on the Application of Conventions and Recommendations, recently supplemented by the *Review of annual reports under the follow-up to the ILO Declaration of Fundamental Principles and Rights at Work.* This compiles government statements in four fields: freedom of association and collective bargaining; the elimination of forced labour; the effective abolition of child labour; and the elimination of discrimination in respect of employment and occupation. The first such review, which covers countries that have not ratified the relevant Conventions, appeared in March 2000.

[25] Considerable detail on these issues and some "naming and shaming" is given in the ILO Report of the Director-General: *Your voice at work: Global report under the Follow-up to the ILO Declaration on Fundamental Principles and Rights at Work* (Geneva, May 2000).

[26] It is true that the excessive proliferation of trade unions could weaken the trade union movement and ultimately prejudice the interests of workers; however, the right balance needs to be struck between the establishment of strong organizations able to develop a long-term commitment to employment, on the one hand, and the free will of workers and employers to establish organizations of their own choosing without previous authorization, on the other.

[27] To the extent that entrepreneurial talent is equally latent in men and women but fewer of the latter develop and use it, gender discrimination reduces overall growth. See B. Esteve-Volart: *Sex discrimination and growth,* IMF Working Paper, WP/00/84 (Washington, DC, 2000).

[28] Similarly, women have spread into higher value-added branches of manufacturing industry. Few easily accessible data are available on female to male ratios of wages but those in the ILO's *Yearbook of Labour Statistics* (of the 1990s) show that, during the 1990s, the ratio for total manufacturing generally rose. The rise was also generally faster for total manufacturing than for specific female-dominated and low-paid sectors such as textiles.

[29] K. J. Arrow: "What has economics to say about racial discrimination", in *Journal of Economic Perspectives,* Vol. 12, No. 2, Spring 1998.

[30] Stalker puts the figure at 2.3 per cent. See P. Stalker: *Workers without frontiers: The impact of globalization on international migration* (Geneva, Lynne Rienner Publishers/ILO, 2000).

[31] US Bureau of the Census: *Statistical Abstract of the United States* (Washington, DC, 1999).

[32] Office of Official Publications of the European Communities: *Eurostat Yearbook 2000* (Luxembourg, 2000).

# THE EMPLOYMENT EFFECTS OF CURRENT POLICIES

# 3

## 3.1 Introduction

Trade and financial liberalization, participation in world markets, intensified competition at the micro level and enterprise restructuring, together with the acquisition of appropriate skills by the labour force, are often spoken of as the economic policy foundations of satisfactory employment growth; the ILO's concerns of non-discrimination and freedom of association are far less frequently mentioned. The former are often alleged to be features of the East and South-East Asian model (although the reality prior to 1997 was very different), which, in the 1980s and most of the 1990s, delivered high levels of employment and output growth in conditions of often low levels of income inequality or indeed of equalizing income distribution. Together with certain accompanying macroeconomic conditions designed to ensure financial stability (such as avoiding overindebtedness) and low levels of price inflation (thereby achieving real interest rate stability), these characteristics have become a common part of economic policy advice. Usually they are combined with injunctions to deregulate labour markets, essentially by substituting bilateral worker-to-employer negotiations (that is, individual contracts) for collective or legislated action. Fortunately, however, full attention has rarely been paid to all these injunctions, which overlook much of what government intervention can contribute to development; certainly, during their early years of success the East and South-East Asian "miracle" countries paid little heed to them. Most countries are still not convinced that full liberalization is the way forward, as applies so obviously in the case of policies on food production, where imports are rarely freed, and is shown in the support for infant industries. Historically, individualistic action in labour market functioning is also generally seen as something to move away from, because of the clear improvements in welfare associated with social legislation.

But this is not, of course, to spurn the features described by the liberalization model. The world is moving towards global free trade, and enterprises must be prepared for competition. But governments nonetheless retain the responsibility and ability to assist this process by, for example, encouraging research and development, and product and process innovation, even if protection through tariff barriers is removed. Macroeconomic stability is important; low levels of inflation are being reached in the industrialized countries, so that developing and transition country exporters must either emulate them through higher productivity or accept a pattern of recurrent devaluation (and the risk of this going out of control) in order to remain competitive. Raising skills levels and improving labour market institutions (particularly those parts of the public administration with corresponding responsibilities) are obviously important if high standards of living are to be achieved. Other basic government responsibilities, such as anti-poverty programmes, judicious investment in infrastructure and ensuring equality of opportunity, although less frequently mentioned, also need attention.

This chapter examines a number of issues related to employment policy in a context of market liberalization. Firstly, it looks at the experience of East and South-East Asia because, whether or not it has been correctly interpreted and the lessons drawn are correct, its stylized depiction in terms of such liberalization has had an enormous intellectual impact on employment policy thinking. The chapter also examines recent developments in Latin America that belie the simple optimism of the liberalization model and suggest that quite different lessons should be drawn from what happened in East and South-East Asia.[1] Section 3.3 reviews the experience of the "older" OECD member countries and in particular looks at the interaction of a deregulated labour market model (mainly championed in North America) with a model of low budget deficits and reduced levels of government debt (corresponding to the Maastricht criteria of the EU). It concludes with a discussion of the so-called "new economy" of the United States. Section 3.4 looks at the main experience of market liberalization in the 1990s – the regime change in Central and Eastern Europe. Some aspects of this are, of course, unique, but what makes the region's experience so interesting is that these countries could not pick and choose their policies. They could not just go ahead and privatize enterprises; they have had to make firms sufficiently competitive so as to create a new economy with fiscal and balance-of-payments equilibrium. In addition, they have had the difficult task of juggling with low wages, extended and expensive social programmes and a poor tax base. In some of these countries, the results have been disastrous.

## 3.2 Developing countries: Recent experience

*East and South-East Asia: What went right?*[2]

A starting point in the discussion of employment policies in East and South-East Asia is to point to the bogeyman of import substitution (IS) policies. For better or worse, in the Asian context the latter is usually identified with South Asia, thus obscuring other differences between the regions in terms of resources and their distribution or enterprise behaviour. South Asia, by and large, chose IS, while East and South-East Asian countries, after a short, initial phase of IS, switched to export expansion. In doing so, they used more of their surplus factor, labour and, to an extent that can be easily exaggerated, set the price of capital faced by entrepreneurs more realistically, although they rejected financial liberalization.[3] The limitations of the "South Asian" paradigm are now well known. The most fundamental point is that the domestic market for manufactured goods in low-income economies is small, and the proportion of employment in large-scale manufacturing, which IS targets, is too low to provide a base for a large expansion of effective demand, based on the home market. Therefore, the opportunity for the expansion of manufacturing production is soon exhausted after imports of consumer goods have been replaced by domestic production, in the absence of sufficiently large increases in per capita income in other sectors. Furthermore, the closed economy, which IS leads to, develops inefficiencies at the enterprise level and in public administration, which can prove particularly difficult to remove. The absence of competition with the world market not only leads to managerial inefficiency but, more importantly, drastically slows down the transfer of technology from the dynamic parts of world manufacturing. In addition, a non-competitive environment is the breeding ground of groups with a vested interest in the augmentation and sharing of "rents" created. All these factors make an IS country uncompetitive in world markets and make a regime reversal extremely difficult and initially extremely harmful to employment and output.

Set against this experience is the record of East and South-East Asian countries moving into an export-oriented policy of industrialization. For two or three decades, this type of development seemed to do wonders for some of these countries. The GDP growth rate of this group was higher than that of any other region in the world. Equally relevant, the degree of income inequality accompanying this growth process was quite low. Some of the countries and territories that first participated in this process, such as Taiwan (China) and the Republic of Korea, achieved virtually full employment and recorded real wage growth at a rate unprecedented in economic history. Other countries coming to this growth process somewhat later, such as Indonesia and Thailand, also experienced substantial growth in labour earnings and a reduction in poverty levels. However, large pockets of low incomes persisted in particular sectors or regions and, certainly in Thailand, income inequality rose in some periods.

The export-oriented strategy has held its predominance in discussions on Asian development strategy for the past three decades. Other South-East Asian countries sought to emulate the success of the initial "Asian tigers", and even the South Asian countries have started moving towards this strategy (in so far as the baggage carried from the IS era allows).

Nevertheless, a problem that many of the export-oriented countries faced, particularly in the 1990s, was their heavy dependence on foreign capital inflows, which financed their high investment ratio over and above the domestic savings available. Such dependence was deliberately avoided during earlier phases of growth in East and South-East Asia. Recent years of East and South-East Asian growth were also marked by an over-reliance on export promotion in the face of overvalued currencies (particularly in Indonesia and Thailand), which the foreign capital inflow helped sustain, and a heavy dependence, on the part of private borrowers in particular, on short-term dollar-denominated foreign debt. The Asian financial crisis emerged as the rate of export growth was being forced to slow down as costs increased and other countries with less overvalued exchange rates became more competitive in dollar prices. With the onset of financial difficulties, short-term capital was free to leave relatively promptly. The downward pressure on exchange rates caused by the deteriorating external current and capital accounts was magnified by the change in investors' expectations. As the exchange rate spiralled downwards, the domestic financial cost of the repatriation of capital continued to rise, which had enormous multiplier effects on the national capital market. Thus the shocks emanating from the external finance sector added enormously to the real problems of adjustment to the economic structure, and a huge crisis emerged.

In this regard, aspects of domestic policy[4] in the region that can be criticized relate both to the build-up to the crisis (in broad terms owing to over-optimism – in the belief that any level of current account deficit in the balance of payments could be sustained – as well as to under-regulation of the finance and banking sectors) and to the handling of the crisis (broadly because policy-makers were not equipped to analyse and develop appropriate responses).This was partly because the institutions needed to analyse policy critically and to encourage the democratic representation of different social interests had not been established. The East and South-East Asian model had also neglected to construct meaningful safety nets, which could have helped sustain consumer demand and prevent social tension. To the extent that "flexibility" in the pre-1997 period meant a "hands-off" approach by government to social issues, it is clear that this was taken too far and involved the neglect of the civil institutions required for good governance. As seen in Chapter 2, some countries have experienced a remarkable rebound, particularly the Republic of Korea, which has mostly come about thanks to large currency devaluations and often quite considerable falls in the price of manufactured exports. Some steps towards greater transparency in government and respect for participatory institutions were, fortunately, taken during the crisis years.

Espousing export orientation as an industrialization strategy is one thing; deciding on the appropriate degree of trade, let alone financial and labour market liberalization, is another. In 1973, the ILO comprehensive employment strategy mission to the Philippines stressed the "vital importance of overall import liberalization and tariff reductions. [...] Without it the general cost structure on which new labour-intensive export industries depend cannot be expected to be sufficiently competitive internationally."[5] Yet countries have been reluctant to accept this advice. Trade liberalization has frequently been avoided by the setting-up of tax-free enclaves and export processing zones (EPZs) as a means to secure export growth. Of the Republic of Korea, T. Michell wrote, in the early 1980s, that "the conventional view is that the Republic of Korea changed from import substitution to export promotion in the early 1960s", but then goes on to show that there was still scope for trade liberalization in the late 1970s and that the pace of trade liberalization was, by and large, determined by the need to avoid a worsening balance of payments.[6] Of course, as more developing countries began to export manufactured goods, the need for their relative prices to be aligned with world relative prices became more obvious and commitment to overall trade liberalization more common.

Financial liberalization and opening up across the board to foreign investment came only later and half-heartedly, particularly in the Republic of Korea. In China, a major exporter, bank lending goes overwhelmingly – and on favourable terms – to the state sector. (As discussed in Chapter 2, it is the private sector that is now creating most employment in China and a reversal of this financial policy is needed.) In many ways, full product and financial market liberalization has traditionally been seen as just one option in the strategy of export orientation. It is quite wrong to identify such liberalization with the experience of East and South-East Asia, which has basically had the common strand of encouraging export orientation backed up by very different approaches to encouraging new industries and skills development. However, the trend in the governance of world trade is towards global free trade, aided to some extent by regional trading agreements. To that extent, competition on all domestic markets is inevitable and there is little support for the protection of infant industries. Competition in financial markets is also expanding rapidly. Since it is rarely possible to turn back the clock, liberalization needs to be accompanied by sensitive anti-poverty, anti-discrimination and skills development policies in order to give workers as much support as possible in meeting its consequences.

On the question of labour market institutions, export orientation was commonly associated with a denial of freedom of association and the repression of independent trade unions, an approach that dies hard. In the Republic of Korea of the 1970s compulsory arbitration in labour disputes in export industries was the rule, although the dismissal of workers was highly regulated. Trade union repression, however, has not necessarily implied wage repression and, as noted in Chapter 2, Indonesia and Thailand made powerful use of minimum wage legislation in the mid-1990s.

In all this, it has been the enterprise that has responded to market signals. One important link in the chain between export growth and income distribution concerns the size distribution of firms. A point that cannot be stressed enough is the importance of having a balance between enterprises of different sizes. Market forces alone do not necessarily bring about a satisfactory balance, because special efforts may be needed to stimulate the growth of smaller enterprises. But experience suggests that intervention policies can easily lead to the excess growth of large enterprises. Given the distribution of employment by firm size, the larger the productivity (and hence usually wage) differential between the different sizes, the more unequal the distribution of wage earnings is likely to be. And, for a given productivity differential, the worst-case scenario for an unequal distribution of earnings is the concentration of employment in only small and very large firms. At one extreme of the Asian pattern lie Taiwan (China) and Hong Kong (China). In these two territories, the distribution of employment is fairly evenly spread across all size groups – ranging from the small (<50), through the middle to the large (>200). In addition, the difference in labour productivity (and hence wages) between the small and large firms is kept to a minimum – of the order of 2:1. This is the type of manufacturing development that is most "optimal" from the point of view of both efficiency and capital use and equity. Not surprisingly, it is also associated with exporting and the production of high-quality goods by a range of size groups, not just the largest.

At the other extreme is India, where the difference in labour productivity between large and small enterprises is of the order of 8:1. India has an exceptionally large proportion of employment in the lowest size group of six to nine workers and an exceptionally low, relative value-added per worker in this group. Certain policies that reserved the production of some goods to small-scale units, together with measures in the financial and labour markets that implicitly discouraged their growth and expansion, led to the creation of a mass of low-productivity small enterprises at the bottom of the industrial structure. These coexist with a fairly large proportion of very large units employing more than 500 workers, of which a number benefit from protection and licensing policies. This has resulted in the phenomenon of what is known as the "missing middle" – a strikingly small proportion of employment in medium-scale firms, employing between 50 and 500 workers. Labour productivity in the middle-sized enterprises that do exist is not so much lower than in the large units in India; it is almost of the same order of magnitude as in Japan and the Republic of Korea. However, the big difference lies in their relative scarcity.

The Republic of Korea began its years of fast industrialization in the 1970s by encouraging the growth of large firms and conglomerates. This was achieved by a combination of subsidized interest rates, allowing privileged access to foreign borrowing and export incentives. This may have been very beneficial in developing new products and processes and in securing export market shares but, as a policy, it began to be reversed in the 1980s. The bias towards smaller enterprises in government policies was not driven by the desire to promote employment or increase the employment elasticity of output growth in manufacturing. Rather, the motivation seems to have been that a shortage of labour and rising wages were having a negative effect on the profitability of large firms. This experience has been mirrored elsewhere; an over-emphasis on achieving growth through large firms runs into problems of high labour and management costs, which ultimately erode competitiveness. Smaller enterprises have to be brought into the picture, either as direct exporters or as close subcontractors. And, of course, there are the distributional implications of the size distribution of manufacturing firms to consider. The degree of income inequality in the Republic of Korea peaked in the late 1970s, when the share of large enterprises in manufacturing reached its highest point. Since then, the inequality index has fallen significantly, along with the downward shift of the size distribution of employment and value-added to smaller establishments.

To summarize, the best policy for industrialization in terms of support for enterprises may change over time. Secondly, export orientation alone can be an ambiguous and insufficiently specified development objective and, finally, although it may not always be wise to be neutral on the size distribution of enterprises, the possible consequences of any intervention leading to a bias towards larger enterprises, perhaps through the choice of trade and industrial policy, need to be carefully considered.

*And in Latin America?*[7]

During the 1980s and 1990s much of the policy advice given to Latin America implicitly had a simplified version of the experience of East and South-East Asia in mind. It was claimed that what was necessary was to shake off the burden of IS and to do this by liberalizing markets. However, the region was urged to this far faster than the East and South-East Asian countries, and, furthermore, in a very different policy and institutional context. In fact, policy advice to Latin America neglected many of the lessons that East and South-East Asian experience had to offer in terms of the benefits of institution building and of public- and private-sector cooperation.

Recent developments in Latin American labour markets must first of all be seen against the background of the economic downturns precipitated by the debt crisis of the 1980s. The cost of the adjustment undertaken (between 1980 and 1990 the region's trade deficit of 4 per cent of GDP changed to a surplus of comparable size) was high, since most countries applied the orthodox medicine of real devaluation and fiscal deficit reduction. All suffered recessions; trade surpluses were produced via depressed domestic demand. The typical pattern involved export growth and real devaluation, with a radical cut in imports. Furthermore, by the early 1990s most countries had undertaken (but not necessarily completed) major reform packages, which included the dismantling of past restrictions on trade and capital flows, financial-sector reform, privatization and other attempts to diminish the size and activities of the public sector, and some changes in labour legislation. The latter changes were generally the introduction of measures to reduce a worker's claim to job protection within the enterprise. However, freedom of association and trade union rights in most cases received stronger legislative support than before. Per capita growth in the region overall averaged 2.6 per cent over 1992–99, still well below that of the decades under the policy packages of the 1960s and 1970s but better than the 1980s. Growth has, however, remained fitful, both for the region on average and for most of its countries, owing to a variety of problems, including the instability of short-term capital flows.

The positive expectations of the (neoclassical) reformers were based on the belief that the previous policies had cheapened capital and raised the price of labour, and had suffered from an anti-export bias as well as pro-urban and anti-agriculture biases. Accordingly, it was presumed that policy reform would eliminate those biases and raise exports and the rate of growth. Agricultural exports (which it was hoped would be especially intensive in low-income labour) were expected to be strongly stimulated, and the removal of the biases in favour of capital intensity would raise the demand for labour at the same time that it increased efficiency. Poverty was therefore expected to fall rapidly through the combined positive effects of faster growth and a better distribution of income following an increased demand for low-skilled workers. The share of tradables in GDP was expected to rise, necessitating a complementary shift of resources, which goes some way to explaining the proposed changes to labour codes, such as the weakening of rules against worker dismissal, the cutting of payroll taxes, etc. The general intention was to increase labour mobility and to diminish the bias against employment of the previous system.

Some of the more general and less cautious statements of the pro-reformers had skipped rather lightly over the possible costs of these policy changes. However, more recent assessments from international financial institutions (IFIs) have addressed this aspect and generally accepted that in the short run the labour market effects would tend to be negative, that is, that the costs would come first and weigh especially heavily on those workers in the market-losing sectors who had little or no mobility to other activities, while the good, new jobs would come along later.[8] It was thus recognized that the informal sector would have to fill in the employment gap in the interim.[9] The earlier, more optimistic, assessments are now untenable in the light of events; the more cautious ones, of a delayed but finally favourable outcome, still based mainly on theory rather than on empirical evidence, are not very different in many of their short-term predictions from those of more pessimistic and negative observers.

Overall export growth (in volume terms) was faster than that of GDP over 1992–99 (9.9 per cent per year against 4.2 per cent per year) but that of imports was faster still (at 10.7 per cent).[10] This combination gives few hints as to whether or not the production of tradables has risen faster than GDP; the fact that both agriculture and manufacturing grew more slowly than GDP suggests the latter. At a more disaggregated level, there are many sectoral differences in growth outcomes, which have frequently been described as an increasing polarization between more modern, often export-oriented, activities and the rest. The heterogeneity of technologies in use has increased, suggesting that the same holds with respect to relative labour productivity. Major questions include the duration of this trend and whether it will ever be self-reversing.

As would be expected, most (perhaps all) of the usual labour market indicators moved negatively during the periods of macroeconomic crises (of which their timing varied somewhat from country to country) and positively, or at least less negatively, when the economies were growing. The more important issue is how well they behaved in absolute terms during fairly successful growth periods. Since the early 1980s, Latin America has, by common consent, suffered the greatest increase in income inequality since reasonably adequate data became available in the 1960s; current discussion and analysis focus mainly on trying to explain the pattern. Why was East and South-East Asia's usually favourable experience in this respect not duplicated here? The timing of the increase in inequality has often coincided with the recessions of the period and with the implementation of economic reforms;[11] S. Morley[12] has concluded that the recessions were substantially to blame for higher inequality, with the implication that, with economic recovery, the high levels of inequality would recede. This factor may have been significant in a number of countries, but it is now clear that an important non-transitory increase in inequality also took place. Where reform coincided temporally with recession, recovery typically did not bring inequality back to its pre-recession level, and in a number of cases where the two did not coincide the reforms were accompanied by jumps in inequality (for example, in Colombia and Ecuador). Much attention has been focused on Chile's record in the 1990s, partly because of the country's shift to a civilian government and partly because it was felt that if the increases in inequality were really transitory, Chile would be the first test case for this hypothesis, since its reforms had been in place the longest. So far, there has been no sign of a significant reduction in inequality in the country.[13]

Various theories have been advanced to explain these increases in inequality. However, given the strong tendency for the main possible contributing factors to have emerged at roughly the same time (trade reforms, other market-friendly reforms, bursts of technological change), it has been impossible to sort out the causal process convincingly.[14] And, of course, compared with most of Asia, income inequality was already relatively high, even in the 1970s. This can generally be traced back to a more concentrated land ownership pattern in Latin America, which may have imposed more segmentation and discrimination and allowed less equal opportunity for its population and labour force. However, the characteristics of labour demand need to be considered simultaneously with those of labour supply.

The main approach to date has emphasized the widening gap between the wages of the skilled and the wages of the less skilled (or educated) workers. A general downward trend in this gap had been occurring prior to the late 1980s, with Latin American countries converging fastest towards the developed country pattern of fairly low earnings differentials, according to E. Lora and G. Marquez.[15] Since then, there has been a reversal, again most marked in Latin America (which also has the widest gaps), with the "Asian tigers" forming an exception as their differentials have continued to fall vis-à-vis those of the developed countries. Thus, while real wages in Latin America have tended to creep up from their 1991 low, this slow recovery has come with a substantial increase in the gap between white- and blue-collar workers, most notably in Peru (by more than 30 per cent), Colombia and Mexico. Lora and Marquez account for this large and widening difference as the result of the low level and slow increase in education in Latin America, of which the labour force currently has two years' less education than the average for its level of development, and four years' less than similar East Asian countries. Years of education in the workforce apparently increased at only 0.9 per cent per year in the 1980s as against 1.6 per cent in the 1960s. The education gap became particularly conspicuous in the 1990s because of the growing demand for skilled labour caused by the upturn in investment. However, as Berry and Mendez comment, it does not appear credible that such a gradually acting force could be primarily responsible for the observed distributional shifts, which have tended to be quite abrupt, often occurring in the course of just two to four years. In any case, D. Robbins's[16] careful attempts to sort out demand and supply effects have tended to conclude that it is demand shifts that most directly underlie the changing patterns of wages and wage differentials. However, it remains to be determined which mechanisms explain the changes in the pattern of labour demand, and how they have interacted with shifts on the supply side and with any changes in the way labour markets have been working.

Reforms in the areas of international trade and investment have been constant elements of the packages instituted in those Latin American countries where distribution has significantly worsened, although reforms have also been present in some cases where it has not (such as Costa Rica). Among the alternative theories put forward to explain an observed association between the removal of trade restrictions and increasing inequality, several[17] assume that the workers involved in producing exports in Latin America are relatively more skilled than workers in East and South-East Asia, with the result that, compared with those countries, intensification of trade widens earnings differentials by level of education. Other theories involve "skills-enhancing trade", that is, the increased capital goods imports associated with trade liberalization increase the returns to skilled labour, which is complementary to capital goods.[18] It has also been widely noted that globalization tends to favour the "large-scale sector" of the economy – large firms, large cities, the more developed regions within the economy, etc. The dominance of large firms in the production of manufactured exports implies less employment creation than would otherwise be expected[19] and is in contrast with the experience of East and South-East Asia presented above.[20] Past IS policies would have accentuated the polarization of the size distribution of firms. Since earnings differences associated with firm size (including those across the formal/informal sector divide) and with regions are often large, an accentuation of this tendency constitutes a real risk of worsening income inequality.

It has been argued that the opening up of trade should raise the relative incomes of agricultural workers, since the IS regimes discriminated against agriculture and especially against agricultural exports. The evidence on this point is still very partial (since household surveys often fail to cover rural areas adequately or at all). There are clear examples of recent labour-intensive agricultural exports,[21] but there are many other examples in which employment creation is limited by the fact that the activities are organized by large farms or corporations.[22] In a number of countries (including Mexico) it appears that a significant part of the agricultural sector cannot easily compete with an onslaught of imports and that the sector's labour resources are not easily mobile to other sectors. The overall story of the impact of the reforms on agriculture and the way this affects labour market outcomes has yet to be told in Latin America. And, at this point, there are few grounds for optimism that the story will be strongly positive.

Confusing the analysis of the effects of the reform packages is the frequency with which large capital flows – either inward or outward – have impinged on the tradables sectors and the economies as a whole. On average for the region, capital inflows in the late 1990s were substantial – at US$50–80 billion per year. These flows would have caused the real exchange rate to appreciate, which may have overwhelmed the potentially positive effects of freer trade.[23] Only when this factor is duly taken into account will a fairer assessment of the other elements of the reform packages be possible. The one component of the packages of which the effects are most definitely questionable so far is precisely this opening up of domestic capital markets. The late 1997 *débâcle* in East Asia only underlines the already obvious problems the unpredictability of these flows have caused individual countries in Latin America.

Latin American experience differs from that of East and South-East Asia in many ways. The area did not have the same diligent build-up of human capital and for long had had a far more concentrated distribution of assets. Government policy on industrialization, while often highly success-ful in terms of creating new industries in the 1960s and 1970s, was for too long focused on meeting only domestic demand. Agriculture, or at least peasant agriculture, was relatively neglected, partly because of the sector's limited political role (even more so than in East and South-East Asia). Economic policy-making was often unsure, with volatile effects on the macroeconomy. Liberalization came abruptly, more so than in East and South-East Asia, and has failed to generate equilibrium in the balance of payments.

## 3.3 The "older" OECD member countries: The 1990s[24]

The so-called "older" OECD member countries (that is, excluding Turkey, Mexico, the Republic of Korea and the member countries of Central Europe) have become a battleground for the interplay of different models of labour market regulation and other forms of public intervention. Many observers place the blame for continued high levels of unemployment in a number of European countries (see Chapter 2) on a combination of factors, including: unduly high wage settlements, exceeding the rate of change of productivity growth; high non-wage labour costs, which render a number of activities unprofitable, especially for low-skilled workers; various forms of legislation on employment protection, which make employers reluctant to hire workers up to the point where their marginal productivity and wage coincide; and levels of unemployment benefits and other programmes that tempt would-be workers into refraining from active job search.[25] To some extent, this list of points (the "deregulatory model") simply reflects aspects of labour market functioning in the United States, which were, at least in the 1970s and 1980s, very different from those of most European countries. The rate of replacement of lost incomes by unemployment benefit and the duration of benefits, the apparent provision in legislation for workers' job security and the level of payroll taxation for financing social security sys-tems all seemed far lower or weaker in the United States than in Europe. Wage behaviour was apparently more moderate in the United States (and in Japan) in the 1970s and 1980s, but, as will become evident, the situation has changed considerably since then.

Two important characteristics of differing models of labour market functioning are the degree of employment protection (basically the ease or difficulty with which an employer can adjust the number of workers, so-called "numerical flexibility") and the extent of wage determination by collective bargaining.[26] However, the degree of coverage by collective bargaining is a measure not of union membership (which is often less than coverage) but of union influence on wage setting. The United States, plus Canada, New Zealand and the United Kingdom, score low on both counts, that is, they all have poor levels of protection and weak union influence. Austria, France and Germany score highly on both (see table 3.1). In between, however, there is little agreement and the rank correlation coefficient for the two variables is 0.56. For some countries, employment protection legislation is strong and may be seen as a kind of substitute for relatively weak unions. In the Nordic countries generally the contrary appears to apply, because in Sweden and Denmark, for example, other institutions and practices exist to help displaced workers, so that legislating for employment protection within the enterprise is redundant. However, overall there is some United States/France and Germany dichotomy, which fuels the IMF's analysis of labour markets, whether or not it makes the IMF's conclusions legitimate.

The United States stands out from the bulk of European countries in two other areas. The first is in its lack of generous unemployment benefit in contrast to the relative generosity of unemployment benefit in most European countries. Features of unemployment benefit include their level, duration and eligibility as well as the extent of retraining or counselling offered and arrangements for income support payments that apply when the unemployment benefit can no longer be drawn. Assessing the whole system in any country is difficult and the measure given in table 3.1 cannot be definitive. Furthermore, benefit systems interact with employment protection systems. Italy, for example, is strong on the latter but not generous on the former. Japan also expects companies to solve their own problems of labour mismatch without resorting to dismissals and has little provision for unemployment benefit.[27]

The other contrast lies in the differing taxation systems of the two areas. It follows from the general share of government expenditure in the economy that the "tax wedge" (see table 3.1) is likely to be relatively low in, for example, Japan or the United States, and high in, for example, the Scandinavian countries. However, the relative importance of taxes levied particularly on the worker, rather than on all consumers, that is, payroll taxes rather than value-added taxes, is likely to change the ranking of the tax wedge by country relative to that of overall government revenue per worker. That the tax wedge is apparently extremely low in Japan and on the high side in the Netherlands suggests that is not an obvious factor in

**Table 3.1**   Selected older OECD member countries: Employment protection and collective bargaining coverage, by country rankings, 1990s

| Country | Tax wedge[1] | Collective bargaining[1] | Employment protection[1] | Unemployment benefit generosity[1] |
|---|---|---|---|---|
| Australia | 1 | 10 | 4 | 4 |
| Austria | 12 | 18 | 16 | 8 |
| Belgium | 10 | 14 | 17 | 15 |
| Canada | 6 | 4 | 3 | 5 |
| Denmark | 8 | 6 | 5 | 17 |
| Finland | 17 | 16 = | 10 | 13 |
| France | 16 | 16 = | 14 | 11 |
| Germany | 11 | 15 | 15 | 5 |
| Ireland | n.a. | n.a. | 12 | n.a. |
| Italy | 15 | 12 | 20 | 6 |
| Japan | 3 | 2 | 8 | 1 |
| Netherlands | 14 | 11 | 9 | 16 |
| New Zealand | 2 | 3 | 2 | 7 |
| Norway | 9 | 8 | 11 | 12 |
| Portugal | 4 | 7 | 18 | 10 |
| Spain | 13 | 9 | 19 | 9 |
| Sweden | 18 | 13 | 6 | 14 |
| United Kingdom | 5 | 5 | 7 | 3 |
| United States | 7 | 1 | 1 | 2 |

n.a. = figures not available; tax wedge = the difference between the value of a worker's output in terms of its purchasing power over consumer goods and the worker's level of consumption.

Note:    [1]Lowest (tax wedge and level of unemployment benefit generosity) or least (coverage by collective bargaining and employment protection).

Sources: For columns 1 and 2, R. Jackman: *Labour market policies in OECD countries: A typology*, Paper prepared for the ILO, Geneva, unpublished, 1998; for column 3, see S. Cazes, T. Boeri and G. Bertola: *Employment protection and labour market adjustments in OECD countries: Evolving institutions and variable enforcement*, Employment and Training Paper, No. 48 (Geneva, ILO, 1999); and for column 4, M. Buti, L. R. Pench and P. Sestito: *European unemployment: Contending theories and institutional complexities*, Document 11/81/98, European Commission, DGII and Forward Studies Unit (Brussels, 1998).

employment growth. Additionally, the size of the tax wedge is another yardstick by which to rank countries (see table 3.1). In fact, it is fairly independent of both the ranking by employment protection (rank correlation 0.33) and the coverage of collective bargaining (correlation 0.63). Nonetheless, the average score of the United States in the three lists is three, compared with 15 for Austria and France.[28]

Features of labour market functioning, such as differentiated payroll taxation or easily available and generous unemployment benefit, can make labour more expensive to the employer, either directly or indirectly, by making would-be workers reluctant to accept work at the rates offered. But there are very many features of labour market operation that can raise the productivity of workers at any given wage level and hence the profitability of employing them. Training (especially in solely enterprise-specific skills) is one such feature, worker-management cooperation in improving work organization is another. Features such as these should offset some of the alleged benefits of the "deregulatory" model. Of course, the bottom line is that the benefits of training, etc., by definition, cannot survive wages rising faster than productivity growth. Training and worker management cooperation are likely to benefit from an environment that favours job security. Therefore, at least this element of the deregulatory model (easy hiring and firing) will cut both ways and a priori could harm as much as benefit employment levels.[29] Training and worker management cooperation play an important role in all labour market contexts, but they are best known as elements of some continental European practice.

It has become an article of faith that, in conditions where the deregulatory model does not apply, the expansion of nominal demand (lower short-term interest rates, faster growth of money supply) will lead only to inflation, and that nothing is to be gained by very low administered interest rates, high fiscal deficits, etc. Structural changes in labour markets must come first. The IMF, however, has accepted that structural reforms are likely to be easier to implement if an economy is run at a high level of demand. But the IMF's *World Economic Outlook* reveals a profound suspicion of so-called "insider–outsider" problems in Europe between employed and unemployed workers and of an alleged inability of European countries to align real wage and productivity growth. Faster output growth, then, only stimulates wage growth and not employment.

This is the link between the deregulatory model and the "generating business investment by low inflation" model. Wage moderation contributes to price stability and in principle aids the accumulation of resources for investment. It is on the basis of an absence of wage moderation that the IMF accounts for the experience, over the past 25 years or more, of higher unemployment levels in Europe at each high point of the business cycle. Upward movements in output are never sufficiently sustained for unemployment to be significantly reduced, because structural rigidities come into play at an early stage (which would cause inflation if interest rates were not raised to discourage output). The type of long-term upswing that the United States experienced after 1991 (which showed signs of slowing down at the end of 2000) has not had a chance to appear in the larger European continental countries. However, this would not appear to be because nominal wage growth has been too high; indeed, falling unit labour costs have been a common feature of European economies in recent years and it is investment performance that has often been very weak. Less dogmatic explanations are also important, including country-specific features such as the strains of German reunification and the particular problems other continental countries faced in meeting the Maastricht convergence criteria for economic and monetary union.[30]

Can clues on the relative behaviour of unemployment rates be gleaned by reviewing data that are more macroeconomic in nature? In recent years, the high unemployment economies have been those with the least successful record of per capita income growth, with, on average, often a positive and quite substantial trade balance, which generally reflects success in industrial exports. Does this suggest that for much of the 1990s domestic demand was unnecessarily depressed?[31] The hypothesis implicitly behind the choice of variables presented in table 3.2 is that countries will expand nominal demand until fears of either inflation or a negative current account balance take over.[32] Of course, problems of timing make this demand management very complicated in practice. The manifestation of official support for nominal demand used here is a combination of varying short-term real interest rates (relative to all other countries in the sample), the change in government debt and the excess of money supply growth over real output growth. Under the Maastricht criteria, government debt levels became a target variable in their own right, thus constraining a government's ability to reflate demand by running a budget deficit and increasing indebtedness. In fact, it appears that: (a) some slow-growing countries, such as Belgium and Italy, were up against a constraint on debt expansion (in both these countries money supply growth was also low); and (b) some high-inflation countries kept real interest rates relatively high compared with all the other countries, presumably in order to dampen inflationary expectations. Thus, some self-denial, at least in the short to medium term, was occurring. Italy is a prime example of a country apparently facing all these constraints. Sweden's position was similar to Italy's, although probably more for cyclical than structural reasons; both countries had large real devaluations. Austria, Germany[33] and Japan had the most relaxed monetary policy over the period.

However, this did not make them the fastest growing countries, which can be explained by a number of factors. Both Japan and Germany saw their real exchange rates appreciate, which might well have slowed growth. Germany was also running into a current account deficit, even at a low growth rate; its price inflation was also above average. Further demand expansion may have been unwise, but very probably the severe structural problems inherent in German reunification set a limit to what even extremely favourable demand conditions could achieve. Japan's problems must have been different in nature, since neither inflation nor the current account was in any way a constraint.

**Table 3.2**   Selected older OECD member countries: Macroeconomic variables, 1992–97

| Countries ranked by per capita income growth | Demand conditions | GDP price deflator | Real exchange rates | Current account | Real interest rates[1] | Government debt[2] | Money supply[3] |
|---|---|---|---|---|---|---|---|
| Ireland | Scarcely favourable | 1.064 | 0.931(est.) | 2.6 | 13 | 16 | 2 |
| Australia | Favourable | 1.051 | 0.989 | -4.3 | 8 | 12 | 4 |
| United Kingdom | Very favourable | 1.08 | 0.953 | -0.4 | 6 | 5 | 6 |
| Denmark | Unfavourable | 1.051 | 1.063 | 1.7 | 11 | 11 | 11 |
| United States | Unfavourable | 1.073 | 1.02 | -1.8 | 10 | 14 | 13 |
| Netherlands | Favourable | 1.059 | 0.979 | 5.7 | 4 | 15 | 9 |
| Canada | Scarcely favourable | 1.045 | 0.866 | -1.8 | 7 | 7 | 16 |
| Japan | Extremely favourable | 1.0 | 1.209 | 2.3 | 1 | 2 | 5 |
| Sweden | Unfavourable | 1.077 | 0.749 | 1.1 | 16 | 6 | 10 |
| Austria | Very favourable | 1.077 | 0.935 | -1.4 | 3 | 8 | 1 |
| Portugal | Scarcely favourable | 1.177 | 0.978 | -1.2 | 14 | 10 | 7= |
| Belgium | Scarcely favourable | 1.082 | 1.049 | 5.4 | 5 | 13 | 12 |
| Spain | Favourable | 1.128 | 0.863 | -0.3 | 12 | 1 | 7= |
| France | Favourable | 1.054 | 0.99 | 1.2 | 9 | 3 | 15 |
| Germany | Extremely favourable | 1.079 | 1.139 | -0.7 | 2 | 4 | 3 |
| Italy | Unfavourable | 1.135 | 0.788 | 2.2 | 15 | 9 | 14 |

Notes:   [1]Lowest. [2]Expanded most. [3]Money supply growth deflated by real GDP (1 = highest). The measure of money supply used is M3. Values for the price deflator and the real exchange rate are the average of changes from the base year, i.e., 1992. The current account balance is an average of annual ratios to GDP as a percentage.

Sources:   OECD: *Main Economic Indicators* (Paris, various years); IMF: *International Financial Statistics* (Washington, DC, various years).

Countries with the least favourable demand conditions include Italy and Sweden, as already mentioned, as well as Denmark and the United States. In the last two, tight monetary policies and a relatively high short-term real interest rate were associated with exchange rate appreciation. Yet it must be assumed that their supply-side situation was very strong, and in part both countries could offset their currency appreciation against low nominal wage growth for production workers.

Countries where demand conditions can be considered "very favourable" include the United Kingdom and Austria, with overall outcomes more satisfactory in the former, where a slight real devaluation interacted very favourably with demand expansion.

Countries with only "favourable" demand conditions include Australia, France, the Netherlands and Spain. Australia was running into a severe current account deficit; Spain had a slight current account deficit and above-average inflation. On the supply side, Spain's real exchange rate fell. Presumably neither Australia nor Spain wished to expand demand further and Australia was doing well with demand conditions as they were. The Netherlands was clearly benefiting very strongly from foreign demand, with an immense current account surplus. Its real interest rate was in fact quite low and the country had no call to expand money supply. France was running a very austere policy as regards money supply; presumably the country had an inflation target in mind.

Finally, demand conditions were "scarcely favourable" in Belgium, Canada, Ireland and Portugal. Ireland nevertheless had a very satisfactory output performance and Canada nearly so. Belgium had a very favourable current account balance but had a debt reduction target and a rigid monetary policy. Portugal presumably had a structural inflation problem and fairly high interest rates.

One or two distinctions should be made at this point. Where the constraint of a balance-of-payments current deficit or a high rate of price inflation occurs, this may signal that demand conditions were as favourable as they could safely be, without changing the structure of the economy through, for example, real devaluation. Where demand conditions were "very favourable" or "extremely favourable" and no obvious balance of payments or inflation constraints emerged but performance was still poor, then one of two possibilities could arise. The first is that demand conditions could have been made even more favourable without running into constraints; the second is that supply is not as responsive (at least in the short term) to favourable demand conditions as it is elsewhere. This is possibly because opportunities for expanding labour-intensive activities are discouraged or, alternatively, because the real exchange rate is unnecessarily high. In this sample, countries such as Austria and France are those where demand conditions might have been expected to lead to more favourable outcomes. And, as noted, Ireland (and to a lesser extent Denmark and the United States) presumably enjoyed such favourable supply conditions that (domestic) demand was almost irrelevant.

It may be recalled (see Chapter 2, table 2.6) that the group of four larger European countries with high unemployment levels (France, Germany, Italy and Spain) have indeed all been relatively poor performers. Demand conditions in the four countries have, though, been very different. Probably in at least three of the four inflation fears repressed nominal demand growth. It is also worth pointing out that the group "EU–15" (minus the United Kingdom and the four countries named above) includes countries with obviously very strong and very weak supply responses to demand. Finally, Canada and the United States have had by no means the same level of demand conditions. It is only because of more favourable conditions that Canada was able to perform as well as the United States (a significant real devaluation in Canada, combined with low inflation, possibly reflected greater wage moderation in Canada than in the United States).

A major objective of the anti-inflationary policy implicit in the adoption of the Maastricht criteria was to encourage business investment, which it was reckoned would come about because real interest rates would be lower and fewer resources would be taken, or bid up, by governments to finance their deficits. An inflation-free or low-inflation horizon should also strengthen confidence on the part of investors. Of course, business investment responds to expectations of (consumer) demand as much as to supply-side factors. Very unfavourable demand conditions are unlikely to be associated with strong investment. It is also intuitively quite possible that very favourable demand conditions would not help business investment if expectations were negative. The investment variable used in table 3.3 is investment in machinery and equipment, which has often been found to be the investment category most clearly linked to economic growth.

In table 3.3 "investment conditions" are a combination of two sets of ranked variables. The first set is real administered interest rates (of which the lowest are considered the most favourable, as in Germany and one or two of its neighbours; low rates are thus favourable to both demand and supply). The other set is the relative degree of expansion of government debt. (A contraction of government debt is viewed as a positive influence on investment, just as it is viewed as a negative influence on nominal demand. This ambiguity is clearly a dilemma of monetary policy.) One further element should probably be the movement of the real exchange rate, since a stronger, appreciated rate could have negative effects on investment

**Table 3.3**    Selected older OECD member countries: Investment in machinery and equipment, 1992–97

| Countries ranked by per capita income growth | Investment conditions | 1997 level (1992/93=100) | 1997 level (deflated by growth of hours worked) |
|---|---|---|---|
| Ireland | Favourable | 124.3[1] | 117.5[1] |
| Australia | Favourable | 184.0 | 168.3 |
| United Kingdom | Scarcely favourable | 123.4 | 115.2 |
| Denmark | Scarcely favourable | 138.6 | 132.1 |
| United States | Favourable | 148.6 | 135.6 |
| Netherlands | Very favourable | 130.0 | 116.8 |
| Canada | Scarcely favourable | 134.9 | 120.5 |
| Japan | Favourable | 112.3 | 112.3 |
| Sweden | Unfavourable | 159.8 | 156.4 |
| Austria | Very favourable | n.a. | n.a. |
| Portugal | Scarcely favourable | 121.3 | 123.1 |
| Belgium | Very favourable | n.a. | n.a. |
| Spain | Unfavourable | 122.4 | 118.0 |
| France | Unfavourable | 113.0 | 114.5 |
| Germany | Favourable | 98.3 | 101.8 |
| Italy | Unfavourable | 112.4 | 116.6 |

n.a. = figures not available.
Note:    [1]1996.
Sources: OECD: *National Accounts*, main aggregates (Paris, various years).

(and vice versa). The table shows that countries performing poorly in terms of growth often had unfavourable investment conditions, while better per-forming ones often had favourable conditions. To that extent, there is some logic in the model that predicts that higher interest rates and an expansion of government debt are negative influences on growth in general. Furthermore, it could be that favourable investment conditions better pre-dict growth performance than favourable demand conditions do. But there are too many exceptions to this statement for it to be very useful. This table and table 3.2 do suggest that Italy had an unfavourable policy environment in every way, and thus the response capacity or flexibility of its labour mar-ket was hardly put to the test in this period. Germany, on the other hand, must have been held back by real supply-side factors, which possibly included the operation of the labour market.

In trying to explain the differences in the behaviour of labour demand, the next variable to consider is labour productivity, that is, real GDP growth over the corresponding change in total hours worked. Table 3.4 shows this for individual countries.

A few countries had decidedly low labour productivity growth, for example, Canada, the Netherlands, the United States (and perhaps Austria), and a few had decidedly high figures, for example, Ireland, followed by

**Table 3.4**    Selected older OECD member countries: Real productivity per hour, 1992–97 (cumulative change)

| Country | Average of values | End years |
|---|---|---|
| Ireland | 1.215 | 1.122 |
| Italy | 1.094 | 1.128 |
| Sweden | 1.080 | 1.113 |
| Portugal | 1.071 | 1.147 |
| Denmark | 1.067 | 1.110 |
| France | 1.052 | 1.122 |
| Belgium | 1.034 | 1.158 |
| United Kingdom | 1.060 | 1.077 |
| Germany | 1.056 | 1.100 |
| Australia | 1.054 | 1.104 |
| Spain | 1.058 | 1.073 |
| United States | 1.028 | 1.045 |
| Austria | 1.018 | 1.052 |
| Netherlands | 1.022 | 1.006 |
| Canada | 1.017 | 1.013 |

Notes:    Rank correlation between the rankings in the two columns = 0.69. Countries are shown in the table by their average rank. The table computes growth both in terms of changes between end years and as an average of each year's change from the initial year. The second seems as helpful a way of calculating growth as simply taking end years and tells more about the stock of work hours and GDP output produced over the period, especially when the series is not at all smooth. However, the ranking of countries is not that different.

Sources:    OECD: *Main Economic Indicators* (Paris, various years).

Italy and Sweden and perhaps Portugal. Most countries, however, had intermediate and relatively similar levels, including some with fast employment growth, such as Australia, and others with a fall in employment (total hours), such as France and Germany. It could, therefore, be claimed that the level of growth affects employment growth, since labour productivity normally comes out at very similar levels. Only through raising output levels will employment grow. But clearly the Netherlands and, for example, Canada have effectively rushed workers into low-productivity jobs, either because wages and associated labour costs were held down to the extent that the activities associated with such jobs became profitable, or because, through market deregulation, new job areas were opened up, largely in low-productivity services sectors. (That the United States economy has been creating both low- and high-productivity jobs is well known and was stressed in the ILO's *World Employment Report 1998–99: Employability in the global economy: How training matters*.) In Italy and Sweden, it seems likely that low-productivity jobs were being phased out.

The deregulatory model of labour markets sees a trade-off between wage levels and employment, and the IMF considers that rising labour demand [*sic*] served to raise wage levels in Germany and employment in the United States. On this argument, Germany chose unemployment implicitly because of the strength of "insider" workers, which led to high wage levels. Such claims can never be totally disproved – it can surely be argued that if workers accept lower wages at constant levels of nominal demand, then that must raise employment, perhaps through lowering labour productivity (changing the employment-generating composition of growth) or through raising profits and thus output (that is, principally through exploiting foreign demand by selling at lower prices than competitors). The links between productivity and wage growth are usually close, though, whatever the direction of causality (Germany's productivity growth has not been obviously high), and can be investigated a bit further by looking at the ratio of compensation of employees to national income as the "price of labour". This is an aggregate unit labour cost and can be expected to reflect the strength of labour demand adjusted for labour supply. The latter variable was identified in Chapter 2 and changes in it are presented, together with changes in the ratio of compensation of employees to national income, in figure 3.1.

The resulting diagram gives scarcely unequivocal results (for the whole sample the regression is poor and not significant). However, it can be interpreted as showing a general correlation, marked by the diagonal, with a large number of outliers, mostly countries that have experienced lower than expected wage pressure. The low levels of wage pressure may be the result of either negotiation or of a move towards increased flexibility in the labour market (that is, a weaker bargaining position for workers). It is tempting to interpret the upward slope of the regression line as suggesting that, for a given level of productivity growth, the relation of compensation of employees to labour demand is very little different in, for example, the United States than in Germany. This would suggest that there is nothing very special about German workers' bargaining power; given the growth of labour productivity and labour demand it is no greater than that of American workers. Indeed, because of higher labour demand, wage pressure in the United States (despite growing inequality) and Australia is, on average, high and wage moderation is, in fact, virtually absent.

Perhaps something can be learned from the outliers. Clearly, the Netherlands experienced far less wage pressure than might have been expected from its level of labour demand (and France, and, especially Japan, somewhat more). In the Netherlands, Denmark and Norway, some deliberate, consensual action was taken to keep nominal wage growth to very moderate levels. For the United Kingdom, the data probably reflect increasing wage differentials by skills level.[34] Ireland is a country where

**Figure 3.1** Relative labour demand and wage pressure in selected OECD member countries, 1992–97

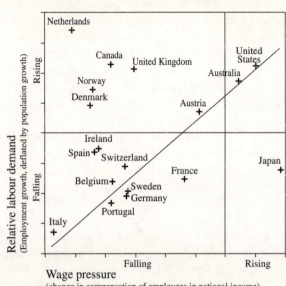

Wage pressure
(change in compensation of employees in national income)
Source: Author's calculations based on data from OECD: *Main Economic Indicators* and *Employment Outlook* (Paris, various years).

some, but in this account relatively modest, wage moderation appears to have been linked to employment growth, not by reducing labour productivity but by raising profits and probably encouraging investment. The most striking outlier on the other side of the regression line is Japan. There, wage pressure is more or less what would be expected from a level of employment growth that took no notice of the fall in hours worked. Furthermore, the absence of any price rise in this period in Japan may have intensified *post hoc* wage pressure.

Labour demand can occasionally be so high that the ratio of changes in compensation of employees to changes in GDP exceeds unity over a period (that is, falls in the top right-hand segment of the figure). This would generally lead to over-consumption and to a balance of trade deficit (which has become very apparent in the United States since 1998). The converse also applies, and both processes could be reversed, partly by exchange rate movements (devaluation cutting consumption in one example, revaluation raising it in the other).

If employment is to grow faster than output, productivity has to fall. In this context, the experience of the Netherlands has to be given attention. The rate of growth of labour productivity in that country more than halved between the mid-1980s and mid-1990s, for very similar levels of output growth. Over the same period: (a) the increase in employment occurred almost entirely in the services sector; (b) the employment rate of women aged 25–54 rose by some 19 percentage points between 1985 and 1997, the second largest increase in the EU (Ireland was the first); and (c) the share of part-time workers in the total rose to over 40 per cent, again the highest in the EU. This can be seen as a fortuitous coincidence of more women wanting to work (and in the Netherlands their employment rate was initially low compared with France or the United Kingdom), of their willingness to accept part-time work and of conditions being favourable for expanding service-sector employment. The European Commission sees scope for increased employment in all branches of the services sector,[35] believes that female employment rates could be higher and that, with more female employment, a snowballing effect should emerge in the form of demand for childcare.[36]

However, it is very unlikely that the conditions associated with a reduced rate of growth of labour productivity in the Netherlands will occur again to anything approaching the same extent. Certainly, there is great potential in many countries for female employment to rise, above all in southern Europe. But a hallmark of the current southern European employment model, although no doubt one that might change, is that very few women work part time. And, even in northern Europe, the incidence of part-time work is below that of the Netherlands, which implies that part-time work may, in the future, fall in that country.

Wage moderation, as already suggested, can no doubt effectively help exporters.[37] (And it must be easier for foreign demand to compensate for the ensuing lower domestic demand in a small country pursuing wage moderation than in a large one, to say nothing of the negative effects on world prices being far greater for a corresponding rise in exports from a larger country or of the share of exports in GDP being larger for small countries.) However, the same effect can be achieved if not through devaluation (which is ineffective if exchange rates with trading partners are fixed, or if any supply constraints operate), then through increased price stability in relation to trading partners. But any form of excessive moderation in comparison either to market-based outcomes or to developments in trading partners when exchange rates are fixed, whether of wages or prices, will probably lower domestic demand relative to foreign demand. The latter, however, is usually going to be less employment-generating, because services are often both more labour-intensive and less tradable than manufactured goods. This phenomenon may have played a role in France, where a positive trade balance was built up without devaluation by relying on price and monetary constraint. This policy may have been chosen because the consensual tripartite institutions were not at hand to produce wage restraint (as figure 3.1 implies).

An obvious problem with advocating strategies of employment promotion that involve the engineering of lower rates of labour productivity growth is that various institutions, practices and expectations are basically incompatible with such a change in strategy. For these reasons, any intended changes in employment strategy should be discussed thoroughly, particularly with workers' and employers' organizations, explicitly to bring out all the implications. Firstly, to reduce the rate of productivity growth means not reducing the rate of productivity growth in existing sectors but introducing more lower-productivity jobs (as is implied in the deregulatory model). Wage-setting behaviour would then need to take productivity growth into account. A fully decentralized wage determination system in an environment of competitive product markets would necessarily achieve this. However, sectoral or national collective bargaining systems would have to take into account a growing variety of productivity levels among enterprises. Such systems would need either to allow more local flexibility (therefore also leading to more unequal outcomes), or be "solidaristic", that is, try to even out increases in wage costs across various activities. However, the latter approach would not help enterprises the operations of which consist predominantly of low-productivity activities; indeed, "solidarity bargaining" in, for example, Sweden in some periods, was aimed precisely at phasing out low-productivity jobs.

Some of the suggestions for deregulatory labour market change cannot be accommodated within an existing negotiating framework because they aim to change essential parts of the framework itself. The resulting hypothesis is that the framework is yielding outcomes that are an obstacle to the growth of low-productivity enterprises and activities. Legislation is then advocated to change, for example, the range of contractual status for workers available, or the conditions under which a contractual status can be altered. Particular attention is likely to be paid to measures encouraging the employment of young workers and unskilled workers (by making it more profitable to employ these two groups). Certain enterprises can be exempted from nationally or sectorally set wages and other determinants of labour costs. Obviously, all this poses some very sensitive issues. The objective is to encourage certain income-generating activities that would otherwise not exist, not to bring about a further change in the distribution of income between labour and capital.

The deregulatory model was set up to explain how employment growth has, to some extent, been higher in countries with the lowest levels of employment protection, least generous unemployment benefit and least trade union influence in wage bargaining. An accompanying model links business investment to growth, and low interest rates and reduced levels of government debt, via inflation levels, to investment. The latter model was taken on board by the EU, in the form of the Maastricht criteria, and is probably turning out to be effective. The former model is not so widely accepted. The link between the two models is through wage moderation, that is, wages rising more slowly than productivity and the primary distribution of income thus shifting in favour of capital. The paradox is that wage moderation has become widespread in Western Europe but is disappearing in, for example, the United States and Australia. Demand for labour would appear to be a major factor at play.

In many countries, the general policy environment of much of the 1990s was clearly unsatisfactory both for raising demand and encouraging investment. Some countries tried to meet inflation targets by keeping a tight control on monetary growth and administering interest rates at high levels. However, indicators of a monetary policy stance are not necessarily an effective guide to outcomes, since, for example, faster-growing countries could afford to repay government debt and frequently did not need to force down interest rates.[38] However, sometimes an apparently very favourable policy environment failed to promote growth, pointing to supply-side difficulties in labour and other markets. Exchange rate over-valuation could also have a negative effect on output growth in such circumstances.

The strategy of achieving faster employment growth by deliberately encouraging the growth of low-wage, labour-intensive activities as an alternative to unemployment and by making low-productivity activities more profitable, possibly by reducing social security charges, seems likely to be effective only in rare circumstances. Indeed, many institutions and practices militate against it. Some notable successes in expanding employment have been based on lowering rates of productivity growth, but this has by no means been universally the case.

The late 1990s saw the emergence of the so-called "new economy" of the United States, which describes the continuation and, indeed, acceleration of growth of that decade into 2000, with no significant increase in inflation. Benign effects of sustained growth and low unemployment apparently extend to reversing the substantial trend towards greater earnings inequality.[39] Over the years 1997–2000 (the last measured using projected values), employment growth in the United States continued to be fairly strong, although marginally below that of Australia and France and much below Canada and Spain (see table 3.5), to take only some of the larger OECD member countries as examples. United States employment growth remained higher than population growth, but not by very much.

**Table 3.5** Growth of employment and productivity in selected OECD member countries, 1997–2000 (three-year totals)

| Country | Employment | Employment divided by population | Productivity[1] | Investment[2] | Current account[3] |
|---|---|---|---|---|---|
| Australia | 5.7 | (1.9) | 7.9 | 17.9 | -5.30 |
| Canada | 8.1 | (4.7) | 1.6 | 18.5 | -0.20 |
| France | 5.5 | (4.2) | 4.4 | 15.6 | •[4] |
| Germany | 1.2 | (0.8) | 5.4 | 15.5 | •[4] |
| Italy | 3.8 | (3.2) | 2.0 | 15.7 | •[4] |
| Spain | 11.5 | (10.0) | 0.8 | 17.0 | •[4] |
| United Kingdom | 3.1 | (2.0) | 4.1 | 18.4 | -1.50 |
| United States | 5.2 | (2.2) | 8.4 | 18.5 | -3.95 |

• = category not applicable.

Notes: [1]GDP growth divided by employment growth. [2]Private non-construction investment. The calculation shows the cumulative addition to the stock of capital (1995–98), assuming the latter was 20 times the investment made in 1995. [3]Percentage of GDP, average 1999–2000. [4]The current account position of the Eurozone area with the rest of the world was a surplus of 0.75 of the area's combined GDP.

Source: OECD: *Main Economic Indicators* (Paris, 2000).

Other countries are also slowly reducing their non-employment rates. However, labour productivity was very high in the United States, so that the past pattern of fast employment growth but low productivity growth appears to have been set aside. In this the United States is matched almost exactly by Australia. Other countries, however, demonstrate a continuation of the old trade-off; Germany has least employment growth and high labour productivity growth, while Spain is at the other end of the scale.

Another parallel between Australia and the United States is the size of the current account deficit in the balance of payments – around 5.3 per cent of GDP (average 1999–2000) in the former and 4.0 per cent in the latter. Both countries have also seen household savings rates fall to next to nothing. Of course, high rates of productivity growth not surprisingly require some evidence of high levels of business investment. This has indeed been high in the United States and Australia and low in Italy and Spain, especially in relation to the increase in employment. However, this difference is unlikely to be sufficient to explain the high levels of productivity growth. Indeed, for the United States more detailed investigation suggests that only around 40 per cent of the increase in labour productivity can be explained by the greater availability of capital per worker and about 10 per cent by higher labour quality.[40] This leaves about 45 per cent unaccounted for, that is, contributed by total factor productivity (TFP), meaning the better utilization of labour and capital. Put another way, if the period 1974–90 is compared with 1996–99, the contribution of TFP to total growth rose from 11 per cent to 24 per cent of a much larger total.

At this point two, not entirely exclusive, explanations arise. One is that the TFP increase is genuine and represents a major breakthrough in the efficient use of labour and capital. The obvious candidate is the increased use of information technology (IT). The argument is that not only does IT raise output as an additional capital good in the same way as any other item of investment, but that it also adds to labour productivity growth significantly in other ways. Purely as a capital good, IT equipment contributed 0.42 of a percentage point to United States growth in 1990–96 (more than double the amount in Germany and France),[41] and S. Oliver and D. Sichel believe the amount reached one percentage point by 1999. It must, however, be noted that IT diffusion is itself likely to contribute to increasing earnings inequality. Indeed, J. Cole and C. Towe find that "the increase in the share of business investment since 1976 [and until 1992] devoted to IT explains just over 60 per cent of the overall increase in the Gini ratio".[42] However, the interaction of computer use, the availability of computer-related skills and changing pay structure is unlikely to be straightforward. Thus, while studies find a wage premium for computer use, they also find one for using pencils.[43]

The other explanation is that the fast growth experienced at the end of the 1990s was unsustainable and was associated with high levels of consumer expenditure, that is, the "wealth effect" of the stock-market boom, large capital inflows and the effects of at least subjective uncertainty about job prospects on moderating wage claims. There was a growth bonus (which is unlikely to be repeated because of the high level of capital inflows), which was obtained at the cost of putting up with the consequences of labour market flexibility for many previous years.

According to R. Gordon,[44] the bonus added at least half a percentage point to growth annually at the end of the 1990s. This still leaves a major increase in labour productivity compared with other countries and with the 1974–90 period (the same applies to Australia where, however, the unsustainable bonus may be larger). Around 40 per cent of the increase in labour productivity in the United States still has to be laid at the door of higher TFP growth. If this is caused by the diffusion of IT use, then other countries can also expect a gain in labour productivity in time, once their overall investment and IT investment pick up. Gordon, however, considers that, in services and manufacturing in general, output growth in the United States can be explained simply by increases in labour and capital inputs, with nothing left to be explained by TFP growth. Investment in IT to that extent had exactly the same effect on output as any other investment, which it complemented. The increase in TFP recorded for the whole economy actually reflected only developments in the IT industry itself. It is, however, still too early to be certain on this point.

The new economy of the United States therefore contains some elements of the old economy, for example, higher investment and higher consumption levels. There is clearly scope for "Euroland" to follow suit and move to a more expansionary policy stance, allowing the current account surplus to be run down in order to raise employment and output growth.

## 3.4    Structural adjustment in Central and Eastern Europe[45]

The regime change in Central and Eastern Europe was certainly not aimed at raising employment levels. On the contrary, from an employment policy point of view it was undertaken in order to make jobs more satisfactory and indeed to reduce the high levels of labour force participation. Fewer but better jobs was the objective.[46] To achieve this would obviously require changes in work organization brought about by competitive pressures operating on enterprises. Open unemployment might or might not emerge, since, in principle, surplus labour could be kept on for some time within the enterprise. If it emerged, provision would be made for positive and active labour market programmes on a socially acceptable level (based on the Swedish experience). Private enterprise would embody new creative forces and be the main impetus to economic growth. Government welfare programmes and generally a high rate of expenditure to GDP would carry on as before. This could possibly describe what happened in the Czech Republic during much of the 1990s, but it does not relate to any of the other relatively large countries in the region. The hope for fewer but better jobs rapidly became a pipe dream. With falling output and incomes, moves away from the labour force (by pensioners), or delays in joining (by students) were rarely completely voluntary. Unemployment emerged, so that the economy's job-creating capacity, even at much reduced participation rates, became an important issue.

The process of transition following the regime change in Central and Eastern Europe began with a severe fall in output everywhere, broadly from 1989/90 to 1990/91. This was inevitable, given that shifting to a market economy required large changes in relative prices (thus making a number of activities unprofitable) as well as a withdrawal of much of the state support and direction inherent in central planning. In addition, the breakdown of many trading relations created uncertainties about suppliers and markets and, furthermore, some countries were already in trouble with their balance of payments. Nonetheless, by and large sustained political changes and the influence of Western governments and international financial agencies have prevented the emergence of serious attempts to return to a command economy. And the very existence of the EU and the likelihood of accession have provided important encouragement and impetus to political reform in many of these countries.[47]

The transition process has proved to be extremely painful for many workers, and for the poorer and less advantaged generally. Restructuring inevitably entailed the destruction of a great many jobs that existed under communism but simply lacked viability in a market economy. Furthermore, many ordinary working people have suffered from a squeeze on welfare benefits, which has partly reflected governments' desperate need to bring ballooning government budget deficits under control, and partly the belief that high levels of social spending (and the high tax rates consequently needed) lower the incentive for individuals to work and save.

Table 3.6, on changes in net material product (NMP) and GDP and trade with 1985 as a base,[48] shows that, between 1985 and 1990, the year following the fall of the Berlin Wall, when Comecon was breaking up, growth was generally positive, albeit slight, even though few liberalization and reform policies had been undertaken domestically. In Poland and especially Romania, growth in the second half of the 1980s was negative, and it was little better in Bulgaria and Hungary (where adjustment measures were already in place to counteract problems in the balance of payments). Conversely, Ukraine's fair expansion in the late 1980s was subsequently totally wiped out. The data for 1993 show how much ground was lost and subsequently made up in Slovakia and how Poland had around a decade of stagnation before enjoying its more recent years of fast growth. Between 1993 and 1998, Ukraine clearly performed the least well. The table also shows exports and imports per capita. Imports appear to have universally grown, which partly reflects increasing capital movements, and shows the degree of foreign competition faced by domestic industry. This has apparently changed little in Bulgaria and Romania. Similarly, a failure of exports per capita to rise significantly can probably be taken as an indicator of minimal restructuring.

In making the transition, these countries have encountered three major sets of problems. The first involves the macroeconomic problems of running their economies and avoiding excessive disequilibria in budget deficits and balance of payments. The second concerns micro-level reforms at the enterprise level for which the principal channel has been privatization. The third concerns the effects of government taxation and expenditure at the household level.

**Table 3.6** Real GDP/NMP and trade in the transition countries of Central and Eastern Europe, 1985–98

| Country | Population (in millions) 1997 | GDNP/NMP 1985 | 1990 | 1993 | 1998 | Exports per capita (in US$) 1989/90 | 1992/93 | 1996/98 | Imports per capita (in US$) 1989/90 | 1992/93 | 1996/98 |
|---|---|---|---|---|---|---|---|---|---|---|---|
| Slovakia | 5.4 | 100 | 106.3 | 82.5 | 107.7 | 830 | n.a. | 1 710 | 770 | n.a. | 2 210 |
| Bulgaria | 8.3 | 100 | 101.1 | 84.6 | 76.3 | n.a. | 450 | 560 | n.a. | 540 | 600 |
| Hungary | 10.2 | 100 | 102.6 | 87.0 | 101.3 | 930 | n.a. | 1 790 | 840 | n.a. | 2 050 |
| Czech Republic | 10.3 | 100 | 106.6 | 93.1 | 102.9 | 830 | n.a. | 2 240 | 770 | n.a. | 2 750 |
| Romania | 22.6 | 100 | 91.3 | 73.7 | 73.6 | 350 | n.a. | 370 | 380 | n.a. | 470 |
| Poland | 38.7 | 100 | 97.9 | 97.0 | 129.7 | 380 | n.a. | 750 | 330 | n.a. | 1 030 |
| Ukraine | 50.9 | 100 | 108.7 | 76.7 | 44.4 | n.a. | 150 | 270 | n.a. | 160 | 330 |
| Russian Federation | 147.1 | 100 | 106.9 | 79.3 | 61.6 | n.a. | 290 | 570 | n.a. | 240 | 460 |

n.a. = figures not available.
Sources: ECE: *Economic Survey of Europe 1999/1* (Geneva, 1999); and IMF: *International Financial Statistics* (Washington, DC, various years).

Data on government deficits and government expenditure as a share of GDP are given in table 3.7. These have to be seen in the light of the countries' overall growth performance. Thus, for example, deficits at the level of those recorded for Poland of around 2 per cent of GDP were no obstacle to growth. Hungary, on this showing, has had trouble controlling its deficit as, on occasions, has the Russian Federation. Bulgaria is the extreme example. Deficits, of course, reflect the behaviour of revenue and expenditure, and the latter is more under government control. Thus, when Bulgaria's deficit was cut substantially in 1997, clearly expenditure bore the brunt. The same applies to Hungary in 1996 and in the Russian Federation in 1997–99. Usually when expenditure creeps up, so does the deficit, suggesting that resource mobilization is extremely difficult and that expenditure control is vital. However, where very severe falls in expenditure have occurred, as in Ukraine, they can only imply cuts in transfer programmes and wage payments, and their short-term welfare consequences are then necessarily negative.

Deficits on the current account of the balance of payments, unlike budget deficits, always require hard financing, and are thus limited by the willingness of foreign lenders to acquire domestic assets. Some countries, such as Romania, have run current account deficits for substantial periods (see table 3.8), while Ukraine has not had that possibility. There is some positive relationship between current account deficits and (changes in) government expenditure. Thus the contraction in government spending in Bulgaria in 1997 was associated with a current account surplus. The same reaction, if a bit delayed, was evident in Hungary. Generally, there has been wide variation in current account deficits, with a need for domestic restraint when they grew high. One way of reducing current account deficits is by changing the real effective exchange rate downwards. In fact, periods of effective exchange rate devaluation have been rare, although it had become more common by 1999. The picture is mainly one of revaluation, that is, a failure of nominal exchange rates to adjust to faster growth in domestic than in foreign prices, mainly because of a wish to limit domestic price inflation. When devaluation did occur, it was sometimes effective in reducing or reversing current account deficits (for example, in Bulgaria, in the periods 1993–94 and 1995–96; in Hungary, 1993–95; and in the Russian Federation, 1997–99) and sometimes not (in Slovakia, 1997–98; and in Romania, 1994–96). Conversely, the large revaluation in Ukraine did not apparently worsen the current account deficit. How responsive economic structures are to changes in border prices and to the real exchange rate largely depends on their microeconomic underpinnings

Table 3.7    Government deficits and government expenditure in the transition
             countries of Central and Eastern Europe, 1993–99 (as a percentage of
             GDP)

| Deficit[1] | 1993 | 1994 | 1995 | 1996 | 1997 | 1998 | 1999 |
|---|---|---|---|---|---|---|---|
| Bulgaria | -12.1 | -4.7 | -5.3 | -19.0 | -2.1 | -2.8 | n.a. |
| Czech Republic | 0.1 | 0.9 | 0.5 | -0.1 | -1.6 | -1.6 | n.a. |
| Hungary | -5.7 | -7.1 | -6.3 | -3.1 | -4.5 | -6.2 | n.a. |
| Poland | n.a. | -2.1 | -1.9 | -2.0 | -1.3 | n.a | n.a. |
| Romania | -0.5 | -2.5 | -3.0 | -4.0 | -3.9 | n.a. | n.a. |
| Russian Federation | n.a. | n.a. | -4.5 | -6.9 | -6.1 | -4.7 | -1.2 |
| Slovakia | n.a. | n.a. | n.a. | n.a. | n.a. | -4.9 | n.a. |
| Expenditure | | | | | | | |
| Bulgaria | 44.8 | 44.8 | 40.9 | 48.1 | 33.5 | 33.5 | n.a. |
| Czech Republic | 41.9 | 43.3 | 42.8 | 41.8 | 41.6 | 41.6[2] | 43.2[2] |
| Hungary | 60.6 | 60.9 | 53.9 | 48.3 | 52.9 | 57.8[2] | n.a. |
| Poland | 50.5 | 48.9 | 47.9 | 47.5 | 48.1 | n.a. | n.a. |
| Romania | 31.5 | 32.0 | 31.8 | 31.4 | 31.8 | n.a. | n.a. |
| Russian Federation | 40.7 | 45.9 | 37.0 | 40.1 | 40.7 | 33.7 | 31.1 |
| Slovakia | 51.0 | 48.0 | 47.0 | 49.0 | 51.0 | n.a. | n.a. |
| Ukraine | 54.5 | 45.8 | 37.4 | 31.6 | 34.8 | n.a. | n.a. |

n.a. = figures not available.
Notes:    [1]No data are available for Ukraine. [2]Assuming the same change for total government expenditure as for total
          expenditure.
Sources:  IMF: *International Financial Statistics* (Washington, DC, various years).

and the speed of enterprise response to the emergence of profitable new
opportunities.

Along with this frequently unstable macroeconomic performance in so
many of the transition countries, there were many attempts at enterprise
restructuring. In principle, the antithesis of state control over productive
enterprises is their privatization, and this has been an obvious and prior element of restructuring. In the Russian Federation, a voucher scheme of
privatization was pushed through in 1993–94. More than 20,000 enterprises were privatized and, by 1997, privatized enterprises accounted for 70
per cent of GDP. But a heavy price was paid for the speed with which this
was taken. Firstly, in most cases it merely resulted in the transfer of ownership to workers and managers ("closed privatization"), so that no stimulus
to greater efficiency from outside owners ensued. Secondly, in some cases
a few individuals acquired control of gigantic firms for next to nothing.
The error the Russian Federation made was to push forward with privatization without ensuring the separation of enterprise owners and employees
(the "governance" issue) and without simultaneously having taken steps to
introduce competition.

**Table 3.8** Real effective exchange rate and current account balance in the transition economies of Central and Eastern Europe, 1993–99 (as a percentage of GDP)

| Real effective exchange rate | 1993 | 1994 | 1995 | 1996 | 1997 | 1998 | 1999 |
|---|---|---|---|---|---|---|---|
| Bulgaria | 97.8 | 89.1 | 100 | 86.1 | 102.6 | 116.3 | 118.0 |
| Czech Republic | 92.0 | 96.7 | 100 | 100.6 | 107.5 | 116.3 | 114.8 |
| Hungary | 106.4 | 104.2 | 100 | 102.8 | 108.1 | 107.4 | 109.5 |
| Poland | 91.6 | 92.4 | 100 | 108.8 | 11.4 | 117.7 | 112.3 |
| Romania | 95.1 | 102.3 | 100 | 90.3 | 105.4 | 136.9 | 116.6 |
| Russian Federation | n.a. | 91.1 | 100 | 122.1 | 128.9 | 114.2 | 80.9 |
| Slovakia | 96.3 | 97.5 | 100 | 99.7 | 104.6 | 102.3 | 99.3 |
| Ukraine | 58.9 | 83.6 | 100 | 117.9 | 133.6 | 130.4 | 126.6 |
| **Current account balance** | | | | | | | |
| Bulgaria | -10.1 | -0.3 | -0.2 | +0.2 | +4.2 | -0.5 | n.a. |
| Czech Republic | +1.4 | -2.1 | -2.6 | -7.4 | -6.2 | -2.5 | n.a. |
| Hungary | -11.0 | -9.8 | -5.7 | -3.8 | -2.2 | -4.9 | n.a. |
| Poland | -6.7 | +1.0 | +0.7 | -2.3 | -4.0 | n.a. | n.a. |
| Romania | -4.7 | -1.5 | -5.0 | -7.3 | -6.1 | -3.8 | n.a. |
| Russian Federation | n.a. | +3.2 | +2.4 | +3.0 | +0.8 | +0.4 | +13.5 |
| Slovakia | -4.8 | +4.9 | +2.2 | -11.1 | -10.1 | -10.4 | n.a. |
| Ukraine | n.a. | -3.2 | -3.1 | -2.6 | -2.7 | n.a. | n.a. |

Sources: IMF: *International Financial Statistics* (Washington, DC, various years).

Privatization in Ukraine has been even less successful in that respect, since around one-quarter of state enterprises were leased to their employees, on terms that gave workers the exclusive right, for three years, to buy the enterprise at its (very low) book value. This was followed in 1994 by a voucher-based mass privatization programme. By 1998 the share of the private sector in GDP had reached 50 per cent, but of the 200 largest enterprises that were offered for sale by tender, only 40 had been sold by mid-1998.[49] The dominant role of "insiders" (workers and managers) in newly privatized firms, together with persistent weaknesses in financial discipline and in the enforcement of bankruptcy law, has contributed to the slow pace of industrial restructuring. In Ukraine, as in the Russian Federation, there are several indicators of continued soft-budget constraints on enterprises: by mid-1998 inter-enterprise arrears amounted to over 80 per cent of GDP and barter trade constituted some 42 per cent of industrial sales. An estimated 50 per cent of all enterprises reported losses in the first few months of 1998.

The voucher method of privatization was pioneered in what used to be Czechoslovakia, beginning in May 1992. Following its separation from

Slovakia in January 1993, the Czech Republic carried through a second phase of privatization, using a voucher scheme that also allowed citizens to hold shares indirectly via investment and privatization funds (IPFs). The theory was that the IPFs would effectively monitor (and enforce restructuring) upon the privatized firms that they owned, thereby exercising the function of "outside" owners.[50] In practice, this did not initially occur, most importantly because many of the IPFs were owned by banks, which led to a conflict of interest.[51] Privatization in Slovakia began before the dissolution of the federation. Subsequent privatization, though, was by direct sales. Prices were set very low, often below book value. The buyer needed only to put down an initial 20 per cent of the purchase price, and was permitted to offset subsequent investment in the enterprise against the balance outstanding. On these terms, privatization proceeded very rapidly, and by the end of 1995 both the Czech Republic and Slovakia had far outstripped other Central and Eastern European countries in the proportion of large enterprises privatized. However, as late as 1996, the gross losses of Slovak firms stood at 8.8 per cent of GDP, high relative both to previous years and to other Central and Eastern European countries.[52]

In Poland, privatization began with the purchase or lease by employees of small and medium sized enterprises. After much political wrangling, a voucher-based privatization programme was implemented in 1995. However, the 500 or so companies involved in the mass privatization programme accounted for only 5 per cent of GDP. Progress in restructuring the banking and financial sector has also been slow. Hungary made a slow start on privatization and did not adopt a voucher scheme. By 1994, the relevant agency, the State Property Agency (SPA), had successfully sold about 1,500 small and medium-sized enterprises to other firms, either domestic or foreign, leaving only a rump of small and unprofitable entities. However, a parallel agency, the State Holding Company, had sold only 13 of the 172 large enterprises in its portfolio and in no instances had 100 per cent of the enterprises been sold. Principally, there was a lack of political will to privatize and, with a change of government by 1997, 75 per cent of GDP was estimated to be produced in the private sector. Given both a decision against mass privatization and a desire to privatize quickly, foreign buyers have inevitably been prominent. By the end of 1996 it was estimated that foreign-majority-owned enterprises accounted for 16 per cent of total value-added. This appears to have galvanized the economy. Smaller companies on the other hand, where domestic ownership predominates, have had a tougher time, facing, in particular, problems of access to bank credit.

Privatization in the region cannot, therefore, generally be said to have been successful. The State commonly and sometimes quickly divested itself of most enterprises (although often keeping control of a number, including those in defence industries). But privatization has often proved to be a sham in terms of change of management and instituting incentives towards seeking profitability and new markets. Rarely has there been a risk of bankruptcy or takeover that would otherwise have spurred performance. Foreign ownership can also provide new management but, not surprisingly, foreign purchases in, for example, the Russian Federation and Ukraine, have been rare.

Because of the prevalence of "closed" privatizations, most firms, in at least the Russian Federation and Ukraine, have put a high premium on maintaining employment and meeting the wage bill. Subsidies (including tax concessions and tax arrears) and inter-enterprise credit have allowed enterprises to retain large numbers of superfluous workers on their pay-rolls.[53] There was no question of producing "fewer but better" jobs. As in the Czech Republic, employment scarcely fell at all, and unemployment remained for long almost negligible. Given that relatively little industry restructuring has occurred owing to weaknesses in corporate governance, it is tempting to surmise that stagnating labour productivity has helped hold open unemployment levels down. In fact, up to 1997 it was the growth of GDP, plus constant levels of labour productivity, rather than stagnating productivity alone that was the key factor in avoiding high unemployment. Other Central European countries saw substantial initial job losses.

What has emerged in many of these countries is a large unregulated sector of activity and employment. This is believed to account for over 25 per cent of GDP in Hungary and 40–60 per cent in Ukraine. Generally, it is high tax rates that drive the growth of this so-called "black" economy, but, as with the accumulation of tax arrears elsewhere, the result of higher taxes is fewer resources flowing through central government. As the black economy grows, the tax base shrinks, tax levels are raised and, completing a vicious circle, more activities go underground. The World Bank had estimated that in Hungary in 1995 if 100,000 workers then believed to be active in the black economy had become fully legal, the Government's budgetary position would have improved by 0.5 per cent of GDP.[54]

Given such a fragile tax base, it seems inevitable that countries should aim at an orderly reduction of the share of government expenditure and transfers in GDP. Firstly, as already noted, the trouble they have had in raising revenue has led to budget deficits that are unsustainable because of difficulties in tapping either domestic or foreign savings. Secondly, a public expenditure share of more than 50 per cent, as has occurred in some years in

Slovakia and Hungary, is almost certainly too high. At this level the benefits at the margin of publicly provided goods, services and transfers are likely to be low, while the distortions resulting from the various tax wedges needed to finance expenditure are likely to be large. For these very practical reasons it seems that transition countries in general should aim to reduce the share of public expenditure in GDP to a percentage in the low 40s.

It may be tempting for governments to clamp down hard on unofficial economic activity, but this should be approached cautiously, as much (but by no means all) unofficial economic activity contributes quite significantly to the overall health of the economy, as well as providing a valuable source of income to many people. The aim, therefore, should be not to destroy the unofficial economy but to promote its integration over time into the official economy. This is best done by keeping tax rates as low as is reasonably possible and also by minimizing the burden of regulation on small firms.

One particular issue is payroll taxation. The unweighted average payroll tax rate in 12 transition economies in 1996 was 44 per cent, compared with an average of 20 per cent in 12 Western European countries in 1992. Payroll taxes (which are typically hypothecated for financing various social benefits) are often singled out as a source of distortion – in particular, they are seen as reducing employment. The traditional neoclassical model of the labour market argues that, if the tax were abolished, the forces of supply and demand would lead to a new and lower equilibrium wage rate at which firms would hire more workers.

However, this is not the only possible outcome, for the payroll tax can be effectively paid by workers. In this case, if the payroll tax were abolished, the wage would rise but employment remain unchanged. (Consumption of the higher wage is, however, at the same level, because a new form of taxation will have been introduced.) Some empirical support for the belief that payroll taxes affect principally wages is that the share of wages in value-added is much smaller in transition countries than in Western Europe.[55] The dramatic fall in real wages in the Russian Federation, coupled with a relatively small fall in employment, also supports this view.

Given some rigidity in wage setting, however, the introduction, extension or raising of payroll taxes may have a negative effect on employment through substitution in production and consumption. The payroll tax would then give producers an incentive to switch to more capital-intensive methods, reducing the demand for labour associated with any given level of output. At the same time, production costs and therefore prices of products that are relatively labour intensive rise relative to more capital-intensive goods and services, giving consumers an incentive to switch from the former to the latter. But probably the most robust effect of payroll taxation is the incentive it gives, for both workers and employers, to move into the unofficial economy.

It is, therefore, not unreasonable to claim that the payroll tax wedges of as high as 30–35 per cent that are falling on employers do distort the structure of incentives and probably have some adverse effects on employment, which suggests that they should be reduced. One straightforward solution would be to switch the financing of health care to broader based income and value-added taxes, provided such taxes can be collected reasonably effectively.

To summarize, the experience of these transition countries is that the first stages of structural reform, consisting of privatization and liberalization, were comparatively easy to achieve; they often had little effect on employment and working relations. A second phase involves building institutions and promoting behavioural norms, including the elimination of a culture of crime and corruption. Other necessary steps include establishing strong corporate governance by "outside" owners, together with effective competition policies and financial-sector reform, including transparency, legal and accounting standards, and effective prudential supervision.

In a recent article, Havrylyshyn and Odling-Smee discuss the various ways in which these changes might come about in the CIS.[56] They raise the possibility that a change of heart by those with powerful vested interests, perhaps in line with a new perception of where their financial interests lay, might occur. Pressure for change might also come from abroad or from the need for more transparent government in order to attract foreign investment. Alternatively, it could come from a strong leader or from the "large underground economy of small entrepreneurs in the Russian Federation and Ukraine, just waiting to stride on to a larger stage".

More than any shortcomings in stabilization, labour market or social security policies, the failure to achieve these goals will result in a failure to achieve a better employment situation. However, faster structural change along these lines would inevitably increase unemployment, and previously hidden unemployment would be converted into open unemployment. To forestall real hardship and any political backlash, the growth of new employment must be maximized. In Poland, new private firms have been the principal source of new jobs, while in Hungary former state enterprises have been revitalized by having been sold to strategic investors.

The economies of the Russian Federation and Ukraine may, however, be already so weak that the poor cannot withstand the pressure of accelerated structural adjustment. Ukraine, especially, is a large transition economy where GDP fell continuously throughout the 1990s.[57] Poverty levels are also very high. Conditions in the Russian Federation are not very different. In these circumstances, then, adjustment requires assistance from the international community, specifically aimed at strengthening social safety nets and maintaining the living standards of the poorest.

## Notes

[1] See the remarks of Agénor and Aizenman: "... the gap that appears to exist between the evidence on the employment effects of trade liberalization (which [...] provides mixed results) and the favourable evidence of the growth effects of outward orientation [...] may be related to the difference between a medium- versus a long-run horizon as well as the difference between the evaluation of trade liberalization [...] versus comprehensive reform programmes." (P. R. Agénor and J. Aizenman: *Trade liberalization and unemployment,* IMF Working Paper WP/95/20, Washington, DC, 1995.)

[2] This section draws on D. Mazumdar: *Constraints to achieving full employment in Asia,* ILO Employment and Training Paper, No. 56 (Geneva, 1999).

[3] East and South-East Asia can be seen, in development terms, as two groups of countries and territories: Hong Kong (China), the Republic of Korea, Singapore and Taiwan (China) on the one hand; and Indonesia, Malaysia and Thailand on the other. The countries' experiences differ in many respects, not least in their degree of government intervention in trade, markets and relative price-setting over the years. The second group of countries includes more recent success stories, with a different experience of asset redistribution, and they have perhaps been more susceptible to neoclassical policy advice.

[4] Aspects of international policy can also be criticized, such as the earlier behaviour of foreign lenders and investors, their reaction to the crisis and the reaction of global institutions to the emergence of financial problems.

[5] See *Sharing in development: A programme of employment, equity and growth for the Philippines* (Geneva, ILO, 1974). This mission was led by G. Ranis and stressed participation in global markets to a greater extent than the missions of D. Seers in the early 1970s.

[6] T. Michell: *From a developing to a newly industrialized country: The Republic of Korea,* 1961–82 (Geneva, ILO, 1988).

[7] This section draws on A. Berry and M. T. Mendez: *Policies to promote adequate employment in Latin America and the Caribbean,* ILO Employment and Training Paper, No. 46 (Geneva, 1999).

[8] This general presumption (voiced, for example, by A. Cox Edwards and S. Edwards: "Labour market distortions and structural adjustment in developing countries", in S. Horton, R. Kanbur and D. Mazumdar [eds]: *Labour markets in an era of adjustment,* Vol. 1, Issues Papers, World Bank, Washington, DC, 1994) depends on whether the industries that lose protection are still able to cover variable costs and hence survive for a period.

[9] International institutions have, with varying degrees of confidence, asserted that the employment benefits will exceed the costs as long as the reforms are duly adopted (World Bank: *World Development Report: Workers in an integrating world,* Washington, DC, 1995; UNCTAD: *Trade and Development Report,* Geneva, 1995; ILO: *World Employment 1995: An ILO report,* Geneva, 1995; and ILO: *World Employment: National policies in a global context,* Geneva, 1996). The ILO has emphasized the potentially negative effects of increasingly mobile capital on labour standards, which, in order to be protected, would require an increase in international cooperation.

[10] IMF: *International Financial Statistics* (Washington, DC, Dec. 1999).

[11] The record of distribution change has been reviewed, inter alia, by several authors. See, for example, A. Berry: "The income distribution threat in Latin America", in *Latin American Research Review,* Vol. 32, No. 2, 1998; and O. Altimir: "Income distribution and poverty: Through crisis and adjustment", in *CEPAL Review,* No. 2, 1994.

[12] S. Morley: *Poverty and inequality in Latin America: The impact of adjustment and recovery in the 1980s* (Baltimore, Maryland, Johns Hopkins University Press, 1995).

[13] See the paper presented to the ILO's Governing Body Working Party on the Social Dimension of the Liberalization of International Trade: *Progress report on the country studies on the social impact of globalization*, GB 274/WP/SDL2, Mar. (Geneva, ILO, 1999).

[14] The most ambitious attempt thus far appears to be that of Londoño and Székely (J. L. Londoño and M. Székely: *Distributional surprises after a decade of reforms: Latin America in the 1990s*, Working Paper 352, Inter-American Development Bank, Washington, DC, 1997). Their study attempts to include policy variables related to the economic reforms, together with other presumed determinants of income distribution, such as the level and distribution of educational attainment, the rate of inflation and the distribution of land. The authors attribute the changes in distribution to an inadequate accumulation of human capital and to the "extreme" increases in the inequality of access to education, a view that Berry and Mendez find implausible or partial, given that the average level of human capital in the labour force tends to change rather slowly, whereas in many of the countries the increase in inequality occurred over a short period of time.

[15] E. Lora and G. Marquez: *Employment problems in Latin America: Perceptions and stylized facts*, Working Paper 371, Inter-American Development Bank (Washington, DC, 1998).

[16] D. Robbins: *Evidence on trade and wages in the developing world*, OECD Development Centre, Technical Paper No. 119 (Paris, 1996).

[17] See A. Wood: *North–south trade, employment and inequality* (Oxford, Clarendon Press, 1994).

[18] See D. Hamermesh: *Labour demand* (Princeton, New Jersey, Princeton University Press, 1993).

[19] See A. Berry: "Firm (or plant) size in the analysis of trade and development", in G. Helleiner (ed.): *Trade policy, industrialization and development: New perspectives* (Oxford, Clarendon Press, 1992).

[20] One issue in the Latin America context concerns those possible obstacles to the growth of small into medium-sized firms, which may be inherent in legislation. Thus, for example, the coverage of payroll taxation depends on the firm size, giving a labour cost gap. Studies such as W. F. Maloney's (*Are labour markets in developing countries dualistic?* World Bank Working Paper No. 1941, Washington, DC, 1998) suggest that the labour cost gap is modest; most others report something more substantial (say, over 25 per cent, even allowing for some of the incidence of the tax falling on the worker). Berry and Mendez (op.cit.) consider that the resulting efficiency loss and the lost employment in the larger-scale sector are harder to judge; the usually lower capital costs of larger firms are likely to act as a partial (or complete?) offset to the higher cost of labour. However, the relative ease with which payroll taxes can be collected, compared with taxes on income or capital, suggests that they are likely to remain. Berry and Mendez suggest that what is important is to ensure that the proceeds of payroll taxation (in financing pensions and workers' and their families' health care) are seen to be used efficiently.

[21] J. Weller: "Non-agricultural rural employment in Central America", in *CEPAL Review*, Vol. 62, Aug. 1997.

[22] See M. R. Carter, B. L. Barhem and D. Mesbah: "Agricultural export booms and the rural poor in Chile, Guatemala and Paraguay", in *Latin American Research Review*, Vol. 321, No. 21, 1996.

[23] Note that Taiwan (China) has usually exported capital, and that for much of the late 1980s the Republic of Korea and Indonesia were also capital exporters.

[24] A similar discussion centred on the 1980s or 1970s would have to consider a very different set of objective facts, which might lead to generally different conclusions. Naturally, concentrating on, for example, the period 1998–2000 would also give a different focus. However, current debates on unemployment require an understanding of developments in the 1990s.

[25] A recent *locus classicus* is IMF: *World Economic Outlook*, May 1999. An additional feature in North America may be greater ease in expanding working hours, compared with restraint in some parts of Europe.

[26] The latter can, of course, be at various levels of centralization or decentralization and it has been famously claimed that both highly centralized and highly decentralized forms of collective bargaining

can yield flexible outcomes ("wage flexibility"). See L. Calmfors and J. Driffill: "Bargaining structure, corporation and macroeconomic performance", in *Economic Policy*, Apr. 1988.

[27] During the 1990s it seems fair to say that benefit systems usually became less generous, pressure on the unemployed to seek work intensified, and more attempts were made to get the long-term unemployed back into work. This help was not altruistic but based on a desire to see the hitherto long-term unemployed engaging in wage competition with existing workers.

[28] The related point – that payroll taxation may become too high for employment growth – is discussed below, principally in relation to Central and Eastern Europe. However, the European Commission also believes that lower payroll taxes on unskilled workers would help their job prospects: "Lowering non-wage labour costs, at the bottom end of the wage range can foster sizeable job creation, especially in low productivity sectors." See European Commission: *Employment and social affairs, from guidelines to action: The national action plans for employment* (Brussels, 1998).

[29] See OECD: *Employment Outlook* (Paris, 1999). Chapter 2 of this publication concludes that EPL (employment protection legislation) strictness has little or no effect on overall employment. Furthermore, the suspicion that stricter EPL legislation helps the employment prospects of prime-age men at the expense of other groups cannot be sustained. However, with stricter legislation, fewer individuals become unemployed, although those that do face a greater risk of longer-term unemployment.

[30] These principally concerned the limit on government debt (60 per cent of GDP), on budget deficits (3 per cent of GDP) and in reducing inflation (not more than 1.5 percentage points higher than the average of that of the three countries with least inflation).

[31] This was the argument of the ILO in its first *World Employment* report. See ILO: *World Employment 1995: An ILO Report* (Geneva, 1995).

[32] The data in what follows are generally averages for the period 1992–97. Taking this period should even out short-term cyclical fluctuations, but may not do so entirely.

[33] This finding is obviously in considerable contrast to experience in earlier periods. However, between 1992 and 1997 monetary growth in Germany (M3, seasonally adjusted) rose nearly twice as fast as nominal GDP, and real interest rates halved. In the United States, M3 rose more slowly than nominal GDP and real interest rates rose to above the level in Germany.

[34] Although wage differentials, especially at the bottom end of the distribution, have been widening in the United Kingdom, they are less than in, for example, Austria, but the speed with which differentials have widened in the former country is very high for Europe.

[35] See European Commission: *Proposals for guidelines for Member States' employment policies, 1999* (Brussels, 1998).

[36] Such institutionalized exchange of services when publicly financed does add to distortions through taxation, so that flexibility in financing and provision is definitely needed. However, by definition, pursuing a goal of full employment does put a separate value (going beyond statistical illusion) on the voluntary exchange of services in an employment and contractual context.

[37] An inevitable question for the Netherlands is the level of importance of wage moderation in contributing to the large current account surplus. There is no simple answer. The unit value of manufactured exports from the Netherlands in 1985–90 fell 4 per cent below that of Germany at the end of the period. However, in 1990–96 the unit price rise was very similar. In the first period, two factors set the Netherlands apart from Germany: Dutch labour productivity in manufacturing rose slightly faster and the currency very slightly devalued; both would weaken unit prices. But these two factors account for only about one half of the behaviour in relative export prices; wage moderation would account for the rest. In the second period, there were no different exchange rate movements. German labour productivity in manufacturing rose faster than that of the Netherlands. That German unit prices did not fall below those of the Netherlands is again probably because of the latter's wage moderation. Thus it seems fair to say that to the extent that unit prices were important in determining the volume of trade, wage levels were also important. However, the differences in the behaviour of unit prices of exports between the Netherlands and Germany have not been great and, of course, a current account surplus reflects importing as well as exporting behaviour.

[38] A recent concept is that of "neutral" interest rates, which in real terms could be 2–3 per cent above the inflation rate.

[39] From 1995–99, real wages of workers in the lowest decile rose by 9.3 per cent overall, slightly faster than those of the top 5 per cent of workers (see Economic Policy Institute: *The State of Working America, 2000–2001*, Washington, DC, 2000). The study also records continued growth in household income inequality and a fall in the coverage of employer-provided health insurance.

[40] S. Oliner and D. Sichel: "The resurgence of growth in the late 1990s: Is information technology the story?", in *Journal of Economic Perspectives*, Vol. 14, No. 4, Fall 2000.

[41] OECD: *OECD Economic Surveys, 1999–2000, United States* (Paris, 2000). There are tricky issues of measurement involved here. United States statisticians consider that the real price of computers has fallen far faster than their German colleagues believe. Thus, the real stock of computers in the economy is that much higher than had they used German statistical methods. The output of the IT industry is also that much higher. The contribution of IT to growth is, therefore, also greater.

[42] J. Cole and C. Towe: *Income distribution and macroeconomic performance in the United States*, IMF Working Paper, WP/96/97 (Washington, DC, 1996).

[43] J. E. Di Nardo and J. Pischke: "The returns to computer use revisited: Have pencils changed the wage structure too?", in *Quarterly Journal of Economics*, Vol. 112, No. 1, 1997.

[44] R. Gordon: "Does the 'new economy' measure up to the great inventions of the past?", in *Journal of Economic Perspectives*, Vol. 14, No. 4, Fall 2000.

[45] This section draws on G. Renshaw: *Achieving full employment in the transition economies*, ILO Employment Paper 2000/7 (Geneva, 2000).

[46] Other employment objectives included real trade union freedom, far better conditions of health and safety, and the possibility of an objective choice between home responsibilities and outside work.

[47] In 1993, the EU made it clear that accession required not only meeting technical criteria but, more importantly, establishing democratic government and protection of minorities as well as the functioning of a market economy.

[48] The data are from the ECE, which has tried hard to make the 1980s data on NMP compatible with data on GDP. For most countries in table 3.6, NMP data were recalculated as GDP.

[49] In mid-1998, Ukraine resolved to speed up restructuring by: selling the very largest enterprises in telecommunications, air transport and energy; breaking up some of the large monopolistic enterprises, especially in the gas and electricity sectors; instigating agricultural land reform and dismantling agro-industry monopolies; and closing down at least 20 coal mines a year between 1998 and 2001.

[50] In forming expectations of the behaviour of the IPFs there appears a danger of confusing three or even four models of corporate governance: (a) IPFs as mutual funds that simply buy and sell shares but exercise no direct control; (b) IPFs as institutional shareholders that occasionally influence firms directly; (c) IPFs as owners with a large enough stake in individual companies to exercise frequent direct control; and (d) IPFs as being like German banks, which, as well as being large lenders to individual companies, also exercise proxy votes on behalf of shareholders.

[51] The normal assumption is that creditors will wish the enterprise to pursue less risky strategies than will shareholders. Furthermore, the counterpart of loss-making enterprises are banks with non-performing loans in their portfolios. Banks are forced to continue financing enterprise losses because the alternative (initiating bankruptcy proceedings) would result in these loans being written off, risking insolvency for the banks themselves. Another undesirable feature has been that the IPFs often acquire "insider" information about companies in their portfolios, which they can exploit in stock-market dealings. There have been numerous cases of fraud, often involving politicians or public officials. Until very recently no independent banking and financial regulatory body existed to check this.

[52] World Bank: *Slovak Republic: A strategy for growth and European integration* (Washington, DC, 1998).

[53] Of course, it is not axiomatic that labour hoarding or hidden unemployment occurs whenever employment falls by proportionately less than output. In most production activities, it is likely that some labour is "overhead" in character, with the effect that even at peak efficiency, employment does not vary in direct proportion to output. By general consensus, however, this phenomenon explains little, if any, of the experience of the transition economies in the 1990s.

[54] World Bank: *World Development Report 1996* (Washington, DC, 1996).

[55] See ILO–CEET: *Social protection and pension systems in Central and Eastern Europe*, Report No. 21 (Budapest, 1997).

[56] O. Havrylyshyn and J. Odling-Smee: "Political economy of stalled reform", in *Finance and Development*, Vol. 37, No. 3, IMF, Washington, DC, September 2000.

[57] Moldova and Tajikistan also more or less qualify. This section draws on G. Renshaw: *Achieving full employment in the transition economies*, ILO Employment Paper 2000/7 (Geneva, 2000).

# CONCLUSIONS

# 4

## 4.1   Introduction

As a guide to economic policy, market liberalization has been adopted more or less consistently throughout the world, and it is fair to question whether it will also help secure employment goals. Certainly, some countries still preserve a large state sector, particularly the Asian transition economies, where prices are not set by the market and companies need not compete for finance and prove their profitability. In the same way, some areas of activity are protected against foreign competition in many countries; agriculture is a common example. In addition, mercantilism is alive and well: many wealthy countries go to great lengths to encourage their exports and to support leading, flagship companies.[1] Nonetheless, the notion of free trade as a benchmark to which other policies should accommodate themselves is generally accepted, and this acceptance also often frees up capital flows. Opposition to market liberalization is often expressed on the grounds of its apparent negative effects on national and global income distribution; these issues receive separate discussion in Section 4.2. Section 4.3 then discusses whether current policies are broadly helping to create full, productive and freely chosen employment in a context of decent work. The final section reviews ways in which the ILO is promoting full employment.

## 4.2   Poverty, income distribution and economic growth

National employment strategies do not operate in a global vacuum. Poverty, in particular, is becoming more geographically concentrated and the income gap between rich and poor countries is widening. The Special Session of the United Nations General Assembly on Follow-up to the World Summit on Social Development, in June 2000 (Geneva), was an opportunity to take stock of world poverty. (Subsequently, the poverty reduction targets that had been set in Copenhagen in 1995 were endorsed by the leaders of the Group of Eight leading industrial countries in Okinawa, Japan, in July 2000.)[2] Taking the rough but, in principle, internationally consistent poverty line of one US dollar per day, both the share and number of poor people in the world fell between 1990 and 1998. Indeed, the share fell in each region but by least in sub-Saharan Africa, where the share of poverty fell by 0.3 per cent annually, which made little dent in absolute poverty given that there was a much faster rise in total population. As a result, the recorded fall in the absolute number of poor people in the world was caused solely by high rates of output growth in East and South-East Asia. Given this picture, it is inevitable that the gap in average incomes between the world's richest and the world's poorest nations has been widening.

How global income distribution develops is a different issue. Measures of income distribution do not just relate to the two ends of the scale but to the cumulative amount of income accruing to shares of the population. As average incomes in, for example, China, continue to rise, world income distribution could improve in a statistical sense. However, income distribution within as well as between countries needs to be considered, which makes the exercise of measuring overall inequality more complicated statistically. The most recent credible data are for 1993 and show a Gini coefficient of 0.66, far higher than is usual for any single nation; from 1988 there had apparently been a slight worsening. However, although a common measure of income distribution, the Gini coefficient is ambiguous; the same coefficient can describe quite different distribution patterns.

It follows then that, in current circumstances, a convergence of world incomes, which would imply the average incomes of poor countries growing faster than those of rich countries, can scarcely be expected. However, it has been noted that income convergence did take place both among sub-regions of large advanced countries and frequently among advanced countries themselves.[3] Income convergence among advanced industrialized countries has been found to be strongly linked to trade liberalization.[4] "Convergence" here is used in the sense of "unconditional" convergence. "Conditional" convergence was noted by Barro (1991), who wrote in relation to data for 98 countries: "Although the simple correlation between per capita growth [1960–85] and the initial [1960] level of per capita GDP is close to zero, the correlation becomes substantially negative[5] if measures of human capital [represented by school enrolment rates] are held constant [...] Thus poor countries tend to catch up with rich countries if the poor countries have high human capital per person [in relation to their level of per capita GDP] but not otherwise."[6] From this and similar findings it follows that social policy is important and can, if correctly designed, help secure faster growth.

Faster growth and poverty alleviation are obviously mediated by income distribution; if the latter is constant, then incomes of the poor rise or fall at the average rate. Initial income distribution is also often thought to affect subsequent growth. It is fairly widely believed that, during the 1990s, national income distribution widened more often than not. This has been already noted for many countries of Latin America and countries in transition. In the latter, an increase in at least inequality of incomes before taxes and transfers was inevitable as wages began to be set by market forces and not by government decree. In China, the Gini coefficient for household income distribution apparently rose from 0.26 to 0.38 between the mid-1980s and early 1990s. In Viet Nam, over a five-year period in the mid-1990s, it rose much less sharply – from 0.33 to 0.35. But in both episodes growth was substantial and poverty fell sharply. It is hard to doubt that the introduction of market incentive systems was not the main force behind both growth and a worsening income distribution.

In advanced countries there is, of course, both pre- and post-tax and transfer distribution of income to consider. In Central and Eastern Europe, the redistributive role of taxes and transfers is less effective than before the 1990s, largely because of difficulties encountered in mobilizing resources through central government. Transfers are apparently also poorly targeted. In the older OECD countries, experience has been quite diverse. Firstly, there has been a very wide variation between countries in the behaviour of the distribution of earnings. In the United States, for example, the dispersion of earnings rose considerably in the 1970s and 1980s but appears to have gone into reverse after 1994.[7] There was also a rise in dispersion in the United Kingdom, but little change in many European continental countries. Indeed, an IMF Working Paper of 2000 has the title, "The unbearable stability of the German wage structure: Evidence and interpretation".[8] Although the distribution of earnings is certainly a major force shaping the distribution of household income, it is hardly the only one; there are other sources of income to consider and families can group together earners from different parts of the earnings distribution. The increase in single-parent households has also worsened income distribution. As a result, overall American household income distribution has not apparently become more equal since the mid-1990s. Faster growth in the United States may have made workers' earnings somewhat more equal, but not households' incomes, and their level of inequality remains among the highest of all OECD member countries.

A. B. Atkinson has pointed out that countries have often been willing to operate tax and transfer systems in ways that offset greater inequality in pre-tax income.[9] This was true of, for example, the United Kingdom in the period 1977–84 and of Finland up until 1994. Atkinson also notes the possibility of a change in social norms during the 1990s affecting both wage policy, which has moved closer to productivity-related pay, and fiscal policy, causing governments to be less willing to finance transfers.

A recent World Bank paper[10] has been widely interpreted as declaring that only growth matters in the struggle for poverty alleviation. It sets out to counter a large number of claims that growth in average incomes is frequently associated with increases in poverty. D. Dollar and A. Kraay's results are that incomes of the poor usually rise in step with average incomes, suggesting a strong inertia in income distribution. Not surprisingly, their paper has generated considerable publicity and it is useful to clarify its claims. Firstly, it compares the average income of households in the bottom quintile with that of the average overall. Clearly, this is only comparing two points on the Lorenz curve and stability in this relationship is quite compatible with many forms of overall distribution. However, it is unlikely that a further concentration of income in the highest quintile, that is, a worsening in the distribution, for example, would be absorbed only by the intervening quintiles, without the lowest being affected as well. Secondly, the paper makes clear that "in terms of growth rates, just under half of the growth of incomes of the poor is explained by growth in mean income". Thus a lot remains to be explained, which, the paper stresses, is country specific and not systematically a matter of national wealth or poverty, faster or slower growth, or more or less recent experience. The adoption of good or bad policies can affect the average income of the poor, particularly, in the exercise conducted by the authors, the reduction of inflation and government consumption. But the authors make it clear that the data do not show that factors such as increased openness to trade or slow growth systematically reduce the ratios of average incomes in the poorest quintile to average incomes overall; sometimes there may be such an association, sometimes not.

One country where information on headcount poverty levels has been generated for many years by household surveys is India. This makes it possible to explain the change in the poverty share in terms of the behaviour of other variables acting within the same time period. In a paper commissioned by the ILO, A. Sen[11] noted that the behaviour of the headcount poverty indicator in India had usually been explained by two variables: the growth of agricultural output per head of rural population (with positive effects on poverty alleviation); and the rate of price increase (which generally had negative effects on poverty levels). However, Sen pointed out that rural wages had risen in rural India, even where agriculture had been stagnant, and he attributed this in part to higher government spending.[12] Sen regresses headcount poverty in rural areas on: agricultural incomes, a measure of commercialization (which turns out, as he expected, to be linked to increased poverty), a public expenditure variable (government expenditure excluding interest payments, defence and administration) and a relative price variable (the price of cereals deflated by the wholesale price index). Adding a real wage variable did not help explain the behaviour of poverty, since real wages responded to relative prices and government expenditures. Sen also noted that, in (an Indian) state-wise examination of poverty, Datt and Ravaillion[13] found that state development expenditure reduced poverty, both by increasing incomes and improving distribution. Higher agricultural output only worked through the former channel, that is, it could not improve income distribution. Earlier, H. Binswanger and J. Quizon[14] had also concluded that, on the basis of Indian data and experience, agricultural development was unlikely to raise agricultural labour incomes substantially, because the use of improved food cropping technologies reduced both relative food prices and the demand for labour.

The positive effect of low relative food prices on poverty is simply that food is the largest item of expenditure among the poor. Of course, where the poor both produce and sell food, their money income is reduced by lower prices unless their food crop output has risen equivalently (and at no extra cost). However, poverty worldwide is increasingly urban-based, and, especially in India, many of the rural poor are not food producers at all.

Government expenditure fulfils many roles. It has always been easy to show that much government expenditure in a wide spectrum of developing countries serves to support existing privileges by being biased towards urban dwellers, middle-income households and people with higher education, and not obviously poverty alleviating. Nonetheless, much government expenditure goes to employ low-wage workers and, past a certain point, any additions to government expenditure may do so disproportionately, if, once other obligations have been met, spending on infrastructure increases. Expenditure cuts could thus have a disproportionate effect in the other direction. And some expenditure will raise the productivity of activities in rural areas.

Where data on the rate of poverty reduction are available separately for urban and rural areas, it does generally appear that poverty decreased faster in the former, suggesting an income shift from villages to larger towns. This was a marked feature in China between 1985 and 1994 and in Viet Nam in the 1990s. It has been increasingly true of Indonesia since the late 1980s, although experience in the Philippines and Pakistan has been more varied. It appears also to be increasingly the case in India. By and large there has also been a trend for government expenditure to fall as a share of GDP, considerably in China and Viet Nam and increasingly in India and Indonesia. Reduced government expenditure has possibly meant that more money is being concentrated on urban areas. As far as the relation of food prices to prices in general is concerned, it is difficult to see any clear trend during episodes of poverty reduction. An exception is possibly Indonesia, where food prices in the 1990s generally rose more slowly than prices in general, thus reinforcing the urban bias in poverty reduction. However, relative food prices have generally drifted upwards in China. Countries frequently let domestic food prices rise higher than might be justified by international prices. (Indonesia was an exception in the mid-1990s.) Of course, many developing countries import very little food and see no reason for domestic prices to be guided by world prices. Nonetheless, cereal imports into many developing countries in the 1990s increased and this may have exerted some downward pressure on domestic prices to the benefit of the urban poor.[15] In poorer countries, however, where most of the poor are in rural areas and are subsistence producers (especially in Africa), it is production rather than prices that is important for welfare.

How much poverty reduction a specific increase in per capita GDP will bring about depends partly on the direction of its income distribution effects, if any, and partly on the distribution of the poor, that is, whether the majority exist just below the poverty line or whether they are spread out more evenly in a downward direction. In Indonesia in the 1980s, per capita GDP growth of around 3 per cent annually was able to reduce the poverty share by up to 6 per cent annually. More recently, the relationship has been less favourable. In Viet Nam, an 8 per cent annual rate of per capita GDP growth reduced the poverty share by around 7 per cent annually. The ratio in India has often been similar.

It is therefore quite legitimate to ask which policies in general terms are favourable for growth. Besides the accumulation of human capital already mentioned, many other micro and macro features have been found to affect growth statistically: levels of business investment (rather than investment in general); government infrastructure investment;[16] trade; openness; the absence of a black-market premium on foreign exchange; size of government; and size of government deficits and their funding.[17] Evidence on these points can be disputed and the direction of causality is not clear. After all, growth can stimulate investment (thus making it very difficult to revive investment after a period of stagnation). And, as Barro has said, if government investment were everywhere at its optimum level, there would be no identifiable relation, and so no statistical investigations could be carried out (and there would be no way of knowing that it was optimal).[18] Growth is also certainly a matter of confidence in property rights, the rule of law and the reinforcement of contracts, let alone of transparent policy-making.

There is some confidence that these last features, which can collectively be called "good governance", have positive distributional effects. In a paper prepared for the ILO,[19] S. Knack noted that institutions which broaden participation and encourage political organization (including freedom of association), as represented empirically by the civil liberties index (see Chapter 1), can be expected to extend to poor people the kind of political influence and access that the rich tend to have. However, the distributional implications of secure property rights and effective contract enforcement are sometimes viewed as benefiting primarily the rich, since the poor have little property to protect. Similarly, contractual agreements may be perceived as the product of unequal bargaining power, with rich lenders and landowners enforcing contract provisions against poor borrowers and tenants. But institutions for promoting secure property rights and the enforcement of contracts can have powerful egalitarian effects, enabling individuals with little property and no political connections to invest in human capital and to build up informal-sector undertakings into small enterprises. The institutions that best ensure property rights and contract enforceability may be the very same institutions that best improve the welfare of the poor[20] and working classes.

It can, of course, be argued that since property and contract rights are usually found to be significantly related to growth,[21] and sufficient growth is usually associated with reductions in poverty rates, such rights will help the poor. However, while most episodes of growth are accompanied by reductions in poverty, the exceptions could be those in which, for example, growth is generated precisely by secure and stable property and contract rights rather than by more common factors such as public investment in primary or secondary education, health or infrastructure. To test this possibility, S. Knack used an international country risk guide (ICRG) index of property rights.[22] He related this to data on income shares by quintile (obtained from the Deininger and Squire's 1996 time-series compilation on income inequality, using the most reliable country data). Average annual growth in per capita income was computed for each of the five income quintiles using the purchasing power-adjusted income data from R. Summers and A. Heston.[23] The results are given in table 4.1.

**Table 4.1**  Property rights index and income growth by quintile, 1970–90

| Standard | Income growth overall[1] | Income growth by quintile[2] | | | | |
|---|---|---|---|---|---|---|
| | 1970–90 | 1980–90 | | | | |
| | | Q1 | Q2 | Q3 | Q4 | Q5 |
| Intercept | -6.790 | | | | | |
| | (2.368) | | | | | |
| Log (income/ US income), 1970 | -2.429 (0.789) | | | | | |
| Mean years of education, 1970 | 0.052 (0.149) | | | | | |
| Trade intensity ratio, 1970–90 mean | 0.010 (0.005) | | | | | |
| ICRG index of property rights | 0.145 (0.031) | 0.266 (0.114) | 0.133 (0.050) | 0.166 (0.047) | 0.167 (0.040) | 0.146 (0.045) |
| Adjusted $R^2$ | 0.510 | | | | | |

Notes:  White-corrected standard errors are in parentheses. [1]Sample size is 31. [2]Sample size is 35.
Source:  Knack, 1999, op. cit.

The first column in table 4.1 reports a standard growth regression for the sample of countries with data on quintile shares. The dependent variable is average annual income growth, over the 1970–90 period or as near to it as permitted by the available data. Independent variables are: (the log of) initial-year per capita income as a share of average income in the United States (for the same year); mean years of completed education; the trade intensity ratio averaged over the period (exports plus imports as a share of GDP); and the index of property rights. Most results for this 31-nation inequality sample are consistent with those generated from larger samples; incomes converge conditional on other variables included in the model, and trade intensity and property rights are associated with higher growth rates. The human capital indicator ("mean years of education completed") is not, however, significant here. The coefficient in the property rights index implies that, controlling for the other independent variables, each ten-point increase in the 50-point scale is associated with a growth increase of nearly 1.5 percentage points per year.

The table also summarizes results from a similar set of regressions for growth over the shorter (roughly) 1980–90 period for each income quintile. These results report only the coefficients and standard errors for the ICRG index from regressions identical to those in the first column (with other independent variables appropriately adjusted to 1980). The coefficient on the property rights index here is at its maximum (0.266) for the poorest quintile, double its magnitude for the second-poorest quintile (0.133) and nearly double that for the richest quintile (0.146). The null hypothesis – that the quintile 5 coefficient is 0.266 – can be rejected at the 0.05 level of significance. Evidence from the 1980–90 period thus suggests that, if anything, good governance aids the poorest group more than higher-income groups.

In the early 1990s a new twist was given to the distribution, poverty alleviation and growth debate by the finding, from certain data sets, that initial income distribution was apparently linked to subsequent income growth negatively, that is, less inequality resulted in more growth.[24] This was an important suggestion, because income inequality had long been given a positive role in capital accumulation on the basis that a (functional) distribution between capital and labour incomes in favour of capital would help savings. On the other hand, a link between egalitarian land distribution, or redistribution, in East Asia and faster growth had long been posited on efficiency grounds. It also appears difficult to disprove the proposition that income inequality is positively related to savings, although it is usually found to be negatively related to investment.[25] The corollary is then that savings do not drive investment (which is unsurprising, since much investment is financed by business from retained profits) and that the indirect effects of income equality on savings, operating through investment and the generation of higher incomes, are significant. It is also disputed whether income inequality is directly related to investment, or indirectly through its effects on political stability, which has an effect on the investment climate.

Explaining the apparent link between income equality and growth has taken a number of forms. One hypothesis was that, in a democracy with unequal income distribution, the middle income group would gain from voting to tax the rich and redistribute consumption. This would allegedly have a negative effect on growth by a combination of higher taxes (which would distort incentives and overall resource allocation) and reduced savings by the rich.[26] This explanation appealed to proponents of "smaller" government. In dictatorships, inequality could simply be a sign of the choice of bad policies and of a considerable temptation to the leadership to benefit from immediate gains and to redistribute to certain favoured groups. More generally, income inequality is likely to be associated, as cause and effect, with lobbying for government support and protection by special interest groups (as has been apparent in some countries' tariff structures) and by significant difficulties encountered by the poor in getting a good education, thus leading to an overall national education deficit. Ethnic and other forms of discrimination could also be important in this respect. Using more precise income distribution data, however, other researchers have failed to find that income inequality is harmful to

113

growth.[27] A World Bank study finds that asset distribution rather than income distribution is crucial.[28] Inequality in asset distribution also has negative effects on human capital accumulation. It seems, however, unlikely that a distinction between asset and income distribution can really be sustained, although the former would encompass the non-distributed earnings of enterprises, which do not appear in household incomes. The distribution of assets will, therefore, usually be more concentrated than that of incomes and consequently bring out the effects of inequality more starkly.

The policy conclusion to be reached from this discussion would be that redistribution, which does in fact strengthen the future earnings position of the poor, is likely to be worthwhile if it strengthens both the relative position of the poor and the prospects for future growth. Education for the children of the poor is an obvious response[29] but nutritional and health programmes can also raise earnings potential. Providing work during off-seasons can prevent a deterioration in health and nutrition uptake. A further argument for redistribution towards the poor is that high income inequality is associated with weak guarantees of the security of property rights and thus higher risks[30] of expropriation, a channel linking income equality to growth.

The two problems with all such proposals for pro-poor programmes are, of course, those of targeting and financing. Targeting raises the issue of restricting the benefits of schemes to those for whom they are designed. Frequently, this is effectively achieved by making the benefits of such low quality that they are unattractive to other groups, which has, however, the consequence of limiting their effectiveness in helping the poor. Financing is an even more difficult issue and usually severely restricts the scope for redistribution, since in the last resort some levels and forms of taxation, let alone inflationary financing methods, can have negative effects on growth.

## 4.3    Are full employment policies broadly on the right track?

The simplest way to discuss whether current policies are going in the right direction, that is, working towards full, productive and freely chosen employment, is to examine some of the major criticisms directed at them. In that way, some solutions may become apparent. They can be listed as follows:

(a) Even if current policies do lead to higher levels of employment, there is often a tendency for national income distribution, particularly wage distribution, to worsen. Also, it is feared that deregulated labour markets will lead to a polarization of jobs and incomes. Furthermore, in many Western European countries the return to full employment is proving to be exceedingly slow.

(b) Radical regime changes towards liberalization are difficult and painful, and countries undertaking them risk ending up in an economic limbo.

(c) Market liberalization largely implies countries losing control over the location of economic activities. "Their jobs" may go elsewhere. Wrongly applied, this can lower working conditions in the original country and, in poorer countries, the arrival of foreign investment is not an unmitigated blessing. In addition, many forms of capital flows into developing countries can pose policy problems.

(d) Market liberalization is not able to prevent high levels of global income inequality, which, at the very least, is a temptation to many workers in poor countries to risk illegal migration and, more generally, is an affront to human dignity.

As far as point (a) is concerned, it is certainly true that wage dispersion has widened in a number of industrialized countries, while overall income distribution has worsened in recent years, in Latin America if not elsewhere. The main reasons (not all of which apply to every situation) include:

- a weakening of the labour market institutions that serve to bring a degree of fairness to wage distribution, including the operation of trade unions, and centralized collective bargaining and minimum wage legislation;[31]

- inflexibility in, and a political reluctance to expand, high-quality education and training systems, leading to a shortage of potentially highly educated and skilled workers in relation to demand; and, on the supply side, obstacles to occupational and social mobility, stemming from gender and other forms of discrimination;

- an inability of small and medium-sized enterprises to upgrade their products to international standards; or a reluctance of larger enterprises to subcontract to small and medium-sized enterprises in ways that raise their productivity levels;

- government pursuit of goals other than full employment, for example, very low inflation or the achievement of a trade surplus, to an exaggerated degree. This has contributed to the inability over the past 20–30 years on the part of some industrialized countries to achieve the decade-long sustained growth which would contribute substantially to employment generation, bearing in mind that low levels of unemployment in the United States appear finally to have reduced inequality in the distribution of earnings;

- the ineffectiveness, or sometimes abandonment, of government efforts to address poverty directly through income transfers, provide high-quality education and similar services to the poor, and encourage worker retraining.

Only the third of these reasons can be remotely described as a "technical issue", although this inability to upgrade products or increase productivity is also partly the outcome of policy choices favouring larger enterprises, as discussed in Chapter 3.[32] However, in deciding on the sequencing and choice of trade-offs between the different objectives of macroeconomic policy (for example, full employment, price stability, running a trade surplus), there is a degree of judgement involved that can be aided by technical expertise gained in economic modelling. Honest mistakes nonetheless can still be made. The other reasons cited seem to be generally a matter of political choice, for example, a lack of commitment to poverty-alleviating programmes, something perhaps not debated or exercised in a fully democratic way. But if attention is given to these issues of helping the low paid, encouraging unionization, and so forth, then the market-liberalization model can have more socially acceptable results and be all the more effective in meeting all the dimensions of employment goals. The point on sustained growth is a difficult one, precisely because some observers suggest that labour market flexibility (and deregulation) and thus probably greater wage inequality are a precondition for sustained growth. But this view is overly dogmatic (see Chapter 3). Economic growth is compatible with many different institutional features of labour and other markets, and has been held back for a number of country-specific reasons.

As far as point (b) is concerned, it is evident that it is difficult to bring about a radical regime change in a socially acceptable way. There is always the view that the counterfactual situation would have been far worse in the absence of change and always the criticism that reforms should be pushed through more strongly. But the difficulties are real. In China, high growth of real output is reducing rural poverty very slowly and, according to the official data reported in Chapter 2 on employment by type of employer, the rural sector has recently ceased shedding labour. In Chapter 3, the costs and likely benefits of market reforms in Latin America were assessed, and the more optimistic approach to their introduction was already shown to have been proved wrong. The major example of a difficult transition is, however, given by many countries of the former Soviet Union, and, for example, Romania. These are the countries that seem to be in limbo.

It is likely that in all these countries a genuine democratic debate on the reform process was lacking, although this could not have been expected under totalitarian rule. In any event, there was probably an absence of realism on the part of the leaders of the Central and Eastern European transition countries and their (international) advisers. It is always easy to say that well-functioning social safety nets should have been in place, but many of these countries had no experience of the effective targeting of benefits and could not afford blanket coverage. Again, small and medium-sized private enterprises (which in Latin America will anyway take up the labour slack) should perhaps have received encouragement, although such encouragement has to be accommodated within a policy environment often strongly influenced by big business.

Point (c) concerns firstly relocation, the export of economic activities that have ceased to be sufficiently profitable to remain in the higher-cost home country. This is part and parcel of a process of industrial adjustment and, in principle, of moving to higher value-added activities as a country's labour force becomes more skilled. Where changes are abrupt, in the wealthier countries at least, there are systems in place to aid displaced workers (such as retraining and job search). Workers may see the threat of relocation as an attempt to reduce certain basic working conditions, including freedom of association, and to undermine the processes of wage bargaining. Even within the EU, where there is agreement on core labour standards, there are fears that enterprises are moving their activities to the host member countries with the least-onerous regulations.[33] At another extreme, some multinationals in EPZs in poorer countries can, and do, use the threat of relocating abroad to put pressure on governments to neglect their obligations to enforce basic international labour standards. This threat has increasingly become a reality in the United States, following the signing of the North American Free Trade Agreement (NAFTA) between Canada, Mexico and the United States in 1993. Shifts of activities to Mexico, for example, are relatively cheap and easy to arrange and finance. K. Bronferbrenner has examined this issue in his study on union-organizing campaigns in the United States in 1996.[34] A majority of employers threatened to close all or part of their plants, very often referring explicitly to NAFTA. With such threats, the success of trade unions in winning recognition in non-unionized plants fell and, where the union did win recognition, in 15 per cent of the cases all or part of the plant closed down within two years, that is, three times the rate reported during the late 1980s before the signing of NAFTA.[35]

One basic response in all these situations is to call for the universal implementation of core, or basic, international labour standards (and for the EU to decide whether its own apparent problems of competitive regulation really call for further harmonization).[36] In principle, all ILO member States should promote the ILO's 1998 Declaration on Fundamental Principles and Rights at Work and its Follow-up. In fact, some trade union movements, especially in the United States, are sceptical about some countries' ability and willingness to do this. They are, therefore, in favour of taking more direct action, linked usually to placing conditions on accepting exports from countries with a poor record on labour standards, that is, giving teeth to a social clause. Unfortunately, exporting activities often make up only a small part of the overall labour market in such countries and are usually not the sector with the worst labour standards record.

The second part of point (c) concerns free capital flows, on which two observations can be made. Firstly, the liberalization of capital flows into and out of most OECD member countries is relatively recent, and can perhaps be seen as an adjunct to the market-liberalization model and not a necessary part of it. Secondly, a wide variety of capital flows exist, depending on the agent (for example, government, bank or financial institution, enterprise or individual) and the instrument (bond, share or bank loan). Different forms of borrowing by different agents can be more, or less, liquid, can imply a greater or lesser shared risk between lender and borrower and can entail risks (of default, exchange rate changes) that can be more, or less, costly to insure against. Prudential regulation should identify the size and types of liabilities that the borrowing country is facing and the likely schedule of repayments. An additional point is that those incurring the liabilities should be broadly able to bear them and be aware of inherent risks. In principle, the concerns of the borrowing country (or country of residence of the private borrowers) should be mirrored by those of the lending institutions in the capital-exporting country. They, after all, should naturally display caution. In fact, responsibility seems often so diffuse that the systems fail. Lenders display a herd instinct and do not dispose of the detailed information they really need. Risks are not properly assessed. Borrowers are apt to be over-optimistic, including in their views of exchange rate stability. The results can be losses on both sides.

It should also be added that borrowing in the financial markets of developed countries can be advantageous (such markets can insist on certain codes of conduct and disclosure of information among borrowers) and that foreign purchases in developing country stock markets can also be a stimulus to local investment. However, foreign financial as well as other agents are often too volatile, both in entering stock markets and, after some setback (by assuming that all borrowers are tarred with the same brush), in leaving them. The common approach to resolving this issue is to ask for greater transparency in the dissemination of information. In fact, a willingness to intervene when necessary on the part of the authorities in the borrowing country and often the application of better rules in the capital-exporting country are both required.

Point (d) concerns global income inequality, which is largely a result of wide differences in average incomes between countries.[37] In general, however, although this may be of less subjective importance (or less important in popular perception) than the changes in the national distribution of income, it remains disturbing. The market liberalization model's contribution to reducing global inequality can only be as good as its income-generating effects in poor countries. Of course, global inequality is a statistical artefact. As a coefficient it can certainly fall, even if the two extremes of the distribution remain far apart, simply if the bulk of the world's population moves up the income ladder. Fortunately, or perhaps unfortunately, this is a real possibility. If the rural poor in China and South Asia do benefit from market liberalization, together with the implementation of the kind of policies noted under point (a) above and discussed in Chapter 3, then countries that are currently considered marginalized will, in a sense, become more so. Inevitably, this is a particular threat to sub-Saharan Africa, where the combination of severe social, economic and market-liberalization policies has generally led to poor employment outcomes. Such economic policies should not on this account be rejected, since they are usually better than the alternative, but they are unlikely on their own to secure steady growth. Aid is needed to provide a better external environment, as well as political stability and transparency.

## 4.4 How the ILO helps

*The global context*

An overall and recent statement of the ILO's recommendations on achieving full employment worldwide is contained in the resolution (and conclusions) concerning employment policies in a global context, adopted by the

83rd Session of the International Labour Conference in 1996, which offered guidelines on improving the global environment for achieving full employment. It began by insisting that countries should "adhere to common rules in maintaining open economic and trade policies and refrain from policies that confer on them an unfair competitive advantage". It went on to suggest that universal compliance with basic labour standards could reduce any protectionist pressures resulting from the threat of domestic job losses in importing countries. This position was further clarified by the adoption in 1998 of the ILO Declaration on Fundamental Principles and Rights at Work and its Follow-up. The Declaration makes it clear that the way forward does not lie in the use of labour standards to justify trade protection. On the contrary, labour standards are regarded as powerful instruments to achieve development with a socially sound base. In this respect, the ratification and full implementation of fundamental labour Conventions by a number of East Asian countries in the wake of the Asian financial crisis demonstrate faith in the practical value of these instruments as means of strengthening the social institutions that build social principles into economic growth.[38]

Considerations of this nature provide the background for the ILO's cooperation with the agencies of the United Nations system. For example, in recent years the ILO has been increasingly collaborating with the IFIs on the analysis of a common framework for understanding employment issues, and the universality of ILO principles is being increasingly recognized at the global political level; the Okinawa Summit of July 2000 welcomed "the increasing cooperation between the ILO and the IFIs in promoting adequate social protection and core labour standards". It urged "the IFIs to incorporate these standards into their policy dialogue with member countries". (It also stressed "the importance of effective cooperation between the World Trade Organization and the ILO on the social dimensions of globalization and trade liberalization".) However, despite such pronouncements, a common international framework for addressing employment policy issues and, more generally, for including social and economic concerns, has yet to emerge. Different United Nations agencies focus on their sectoral concerns, and there is no perspective within which agreement can be reached on the weight to be given to achieving different policy objectives. Full employment is accepted as a major policy objective, but actual or imagined trade-offs between that and other objectives are weighed differently.

When a common United Nations framework for social and economic policy does emerge, social dialogue will be a key component in its implementation. To this end, it is necessary to increase tripartite contributions to the policy advice given by the IMF and the World Bank. At the national level there is a corresponding need to upgrade the capacity and competence of employers' and workers' organizations. To bring that about requires increased action and assistance by the ILO, and also a commitment by national governments to share information with the social partners and to demonstrate that governments value their contribution to debate.

*At the national level*

A vehicle by which the ILO gives advice on employment policies – and one given greater weight since the 1995 World Summit for Social Development – is that of country employment policy reviews (CEPRs). These reviews provide support to governments, and employers' and workers' organizations in formulating policies and programmes leading to full employment with full respect for workers' rights, thereby also covering issues of child labour and gender equality. In this way, CEPRs assist governments in giving substance to their commitment made at the World Summit to promote the goal of full employment and quality employment through an appropriate choice of economic and social policies, as well as through the establishment of efficient institutions and the necessary legal framework. ILO teams work with governments and the social partners in assessing the nature of the country's employment and labour situation and identifying the principal problems to be solved. In a second phase, teams assist the national authorities in evaluating the impact of existing policies and programmes on employment creation and on the quality of employment; at this stage new or improved policies and programmes can be proposed. Naturally, representatives of the social partners are involved in framing any such new proposals. Proposals are also sometimes made for better employment monitoring and evaluation systems, including developing the machinery for new data collection. All reviews culminate in a tripartite national conference in order to publicize and reinforce the public authorities' commitment to the promotion of full employment and to ensure the support of the social partners for newly agreed initiatives.

As a universal organization, the ILO must base its policy advice to its constituents on a common set of principles, even though ILO instruments frequently underline the need to pay attention to countries' level of development and special circumstances. In the field of employment policy, and in addition to ensuring freedom of association, overcoming discrimination, and eliminating forced labour and the worst forms of child labour, certain areas fall squarely within the ILO's competence and have been the subject of consensual agreement in its policy-making bodies. These include: developing workers' skills and capabilities; job creation in small and medium-sized enterprises and in the informal sector; labour market flexibility, employment protection and security; wage determination; and work and family life.

The ILO's principles on improving workers' skills and capabilities are contained in the Human Resources Development Convention, 1975 (No. 142), and its accompanying Recommendation (No. 150).[39] Convention No. 142 restates the principle of equal opportunity and non-discrimination in training. This is of major importance, both because women customarily receive less training than men and because migrant workers and workers from ethnic minorities are likely to be recruited for, and remain in, low-productivity jobs. Recommendation No. 150 goes further by suggesting that countries should have a vocational training system and use it to help groups of the population that are economically or socially disadvantaged. New labour force entrants should receive general education coordinated with practical training, basic training in skills common to several occupations, and specialization as preparation for an already existing job. Employers should establish plans for the further training of all their workers. Such continuing vocational training might receive public financial support. Work that meets certain standards of quality would lead to a qualification, which should also take into account work experience in the occupation. Standards should be reviewed periodically and their applicability extended until all major occupations and all levels of skill and responsibility are covered. The Recommendation neither assumes nor rejects the notion that a training system should be publicly financed. It notes that employers may be reluctant to engage in further training and suggests that part of the cost might be borne publicly. An alternative would be to impose a training levy on employers who fail to carry out a specific degree of training and to refund it according to the training they undertake. The Recommendation clearly comes down in favour of universal certification, which indeed seems to be a precondition for establishing a training culture, and the full use of acquired qualifications in recruiting new workers.

More emphasis is currently being placed on the concept of partnership in training, as a means of clarifying to some extent the respective roles of governments, employers and workers. Governments are now less the direct providers of training and more the facilitators and joint designers of training policy, which means taking a long-term perspective.

The Job Creation in Small and Medium-sized Enterprises Recommendation, 1998 (No. 189), sets out the ILO's approach to policy advice in this area. It is based on five principles: (a) equal opportunities for enterprises of all sizes and types, and equal access to credit and capital markets, goods markets, information and technical skills, and the application of fair taxation; (b) non-discriminatory application of labour legislation; (c) the observance of international labour standards related to child labour; (d) the promotion of tripartite mechanisms to review policies on small enterprises and tripartite involvement in programmes to develop business services; and (e) the upgrading of the informal sector so that it becomes part of the organized sector. Governments should examine whether social protection extends to workers in small enterprises and whether compliance is assured in areas such as medical care, sickness, unemployment, old age, employment injury and family, maternity, invalidity and survivor benefits. Governments should check that labour and social legislation meets the needs of small and medium-sized enterprises as well as ensuring adequate protection and working conditions for workers. Given this, they should take steps to develop entrepreneurial attitudes and encourage a positive attitude to risk-taking and to lifelong learning on the part of workers and entrepreneurs. An effective service infrastructure to aid the development of small and medium-sized enterprises should be set up.

The Recommendation mentions the need to assist the informal sector to become part of the organized sector and notes that administrative requirements imposed on small enterprises can be overly burdensome. However, easing such requirements should not prejudice the level of conditions of work. In this respect, ILO policy still faces the dilemma recognized by the Employment Policy (Supplementary Provisions) Recommendation, 1984 (No. 169): "Members should take into account that integration of the informal sector with the formal sector may reduce its ability to absorb labour and generate income. Nevertheless they should seek progressively to extend measures of regulation to the informal sector".

Recently, there have been many changes in the structure of employment in terms of labour market flexibility that have largely emerged thanks to global competitive pressures. The resolution (and conclusions) concerning employment policies in a global context, adopted by the 83rd Session of the International Labour Conference in 1996, described such structural changes as including–

... new forms of flexible employment, a higher turnover of jobs, and a growing trend towards shorter and flexible working time. In consequence new policies for ensuring employment security, social protection and labour market flexibility need to be developed. [...] These include the enhancement of employability security through expanded opportunities for lifelong training and retraining.

The resolution also mentioned the need to "combine employment security and flexibility in the utilization of labour through, amongst other means, collective bargaining on the reorganization of work and investment in appropriate skills".

One response towards ensuring employability is through training and retraining, ideally without the worker experiencing a spell of unemployment, that is, emphasizing skills upgrading within the enterprise. One aspect of employment security is that of employment termination. The Termination of Employment Convention, 1982 (No. 158), specifically permits the exclusion from its provisions of workers engaged for a specified period of time or a specified task, and workers engaged on a casual basis. The accompanying Termination of Employment Recommendation, 1982 (No. 166), tries to restrict the use of these clauses by suggesting that the renewal of a contract for a specified period of time should be deemed to be an open-ended contract. ILO policy is therefore sceptical about the acceptability of achieving labour market flexibility through a series of time- or job-based contracts. In addition, other instruments specify that neither part-time workers nor homeworkers should receive treatment different to that accorded to regular full-time workers in regard to employment security.

The role of social dialogue and of achieving flexibility through collective bargaining was specifically mentioned in an 1996 International Labour Conference resolution. Collective bargaining may, in this respect, have the greatest scope for negotiating flexibility in matters relating to hours worked (whether weekly, monthly or annually) and work organization, although legislative changes may, in many cases, first be needed. However, the mention of collective bargaining is to be seen in contrast to the use of individually negotiated contracts, specifying terms and conditions of employment. ILO policy is that legislation and collective bargaining have an important role to play in ensuring that individual workers do not have to agree to any and all terms of conditions of employment.

A further issue is that some employees are engaged in working relationships with no employment contract at all, that is, they are on the borderline between independence (as a self-employed person providing a service) and an employment relationship. Some of this may even take place in public sector job-creation activities. ILO policy is that, as a general rule, an employment relationship should be regularized if it is generally felt to exist.

A major function of collective bargaining is, of course, wage determination. This is a difficult area in which to obtain tripartite consensus, and the ILO has not attempted to produce an instrument on determining wage levels, apart from the Minimum Wage Fixing Convention, 1970 (No. 131).

(This sets out the desirable procedures for setting minimum wages.) There is, of course, the stated right to equal remuneration of men and women for work of equal value, and a further aspect of ILO policy relating to wages is the inviolability of freely negotiated wages to revision by public policy.

The ILO Governing Body Committee on Employment (since renamed the Committee on Employment and Social Policy) reached a consensus on a broad set of issues in the field, published by the ILO in 1992 as *Wages policy: Wages and non-labour costs and their relation to employment under conditions of structural adjustment*. Some of the points that emerged at that time and which received general agreement are as follows: minimum wages have an important role to play in providing safety net protection for the lowest income groups; by devoting careful attention to the provision and targeting of state-provided social services, the pressure for wage increases may be moderated; wage differentials have an important role to play in facilitating enhanced labour mobility between contracting and expanding firms and industries; caution may be required when altering wage differentials within an enterprise; and the implementation and success of performance-related pay have been enhanced when linked to increased worker participation in management.

Some of these points should be seen in conjunction with what was stated earlier, namely that wage differentials within an enterprise are not just a matter for the individual worker and the employer but for all workers because of their concern about "fairness" of treatment. The inclusion of the notion of a "social wage", that is, a complementarity between the employer's payments to a worker and the state-provided services enjoyed by workers and their dependants, is important. It explicitly opens the way for national-level tripartite agreements (since the provision of social services makes no distinction by industry or occupation). It also has a gender dimension if the services provided are, for example, childcare facilities. Such agreements, often involving nominal wage restraint as a component of a larger, agreed package, have been an important element in the employment policies of some of the countries that have successfully expanded jobs (see Chapter 3).

A number of issues in relation to the gender distribution of employment (noted in Chapter 2) are relevant to policies reconciling the demands of work and family life. Firstly, in many parts of the world more women but fewer men are working. Secondly, in transition countries there has been a fall in women's labour force participation and, with a changing approach to previously state-owned enterprises, fewer communal childcare and other facilities are being provided. Thirdly, in some poorer countries women are working longer hours in order to compensate for the State's inability to pay for their children's education, and in some wealthier countries less-skilled women are working longer hours, partly because their wages have been stagnating or falling and partly because their partners are either unemployed or earning less than before. Finally, in some instances all family members of working age are unemployed, with understandably severe consequences for household income and child welfare.

In approaching policy in this area, two elements need to be considered. The first concerns equality of opportunity, equal pay for work of equal value and the elimination of all forms of gender discrimination. Women and men should compete and cooperate in work on equal terms. A second element is given by the ILO's Workers with Family Responsibilities Convention, 1981 (No. 156). "Family responsibilities" refer to responsibilities to dependent children or to other immediate family members where such responsibilities "restrict their [the workers'] possibilities of preparing for, entering, participating in or advancing in economic activity". National policies should enable people with family responsibilities who wish to work to do so without any conflict arising. The Convention mentions the development and promotion of childcare and "family services and facilities". Governments should also take measures to allow workers to re-enter the labour force after an absence owing to family responsibilities. Further detail is given in the accompanying Workers with Family Responsibilities Recommendation, 1981 (No. 156), which pays particular attention to part-time, temporary and home workers.

Convention No. 156 was adopted at a time when more women were working but before high levels of unemployment appeared in many industrialized countries. It basically presupposes the existence of the family, and hence the likelihood of dependent children, and seeks to concentrate attention on combining greater work outside the household with the care of dependants. It says nothing of the situation of single-parent households or of households with no working members.

The ILO is committed to continuing to stress the importance of a number of principles. Foremost are those included in the 1998 Declaration on Fundamental Principles and Rights at Work and its Follow-up, namely freedom of association and the right to collective bargaining, the abolition of forced labour, the elimination of many forms of child labour, and non-discrimination. These, when properly implemented, can contribute to harmonious development, the prevention of economic crises, the mitigation of social pain, the creation of decent jobs and the integration of social with economic concerns. The ILO will continue to highlight the need to abolish all forms of child labour, especially the worst forms, identified and condemned in the Worst Forms of Child Labour Convention, 1999 (No.

182). It will also stress that special efforts are needed to give the greatest possible emphasis to the recruitment of women, to their training and promotion and to their representation within organizations of workers and employers, and, through labour market policies, to ensure that gender segregation does not herald discriminatory treatment.

The main thrust of the ILO's view of the way forward combines freedom of association, the promotion of social dialogue and the integration of social and employment issues on an equal footing with output growth. The modalities by which this vision can be built into practical policies are the subject of constant debate. They require a recognition of the benefits that competitive market forces can bring in liberating creativity and innovation, as well as the need for regulation and democratic participation to avoid exploitation and to ensure equal opportunities.

## Notes

[1] Stiglitz attributes much of this to politicians seeing economic policy as a zero-sum game. He writes: "Nowhere is the problem greater than in the area of international trade [...] At one Congressional hearing, a Senator asked if each $1 billion of exports created 20–25,000 jobs, then would not $1 billion of imports cost 20-25,000 jobs [...] what I pointed out was that the economic justification for free trade is not that it creates jobs – that is a matter for macroeconomic policy combined with flexible labour and product markets – but that it allows us to take advantage of our comparative advantage." See J. Stiglitz: "Distinguished lecture on economics in government: The private uses of public interests, incentives and institutions", in *Journal of Economic Perspectives*, Vol. 12, No. 2, Spring 1998.

[2] Their communiqué included the following: "We commit ourselves to the agreed international development goals, including the overarching objective of reducing the share of the world's population living in extreme poverty to half its 1990 level by 2015." Oxfam has shown that current trends are not sufficient to achieve this (Oxfam Policy Papers: *Missing the target*, 6/00).

[3] X. X. Sala-i-Martin: "Regional cohesion: Evidence and theories of regional growth and convergence", in *European Economic Review*, Vol. 40, No. 6, 1996.

[4] D. Ben-David: "Equalizing exchange: Trade liberalization and income convergence", in *Quarterly Journal of Economics*, Vol. CVIII, Issue 3, 1993.

[5] That is, initially lower-income countries grow faster.

[6] R. J. Barro: "Economic growth in a cross-section of countries", in *Quarterly Journal of Economics*, Vol. CVI, Issue 2, 1991.

[7] J. Galbraith and V. Garza Cantu: *Inequality in American manufacturing wages, 1920–1998: A revised estimate* (University of Texas Inequality Project, 1999).

[8] E. S. Prasad (IMF, Washington, DC, WP 00/22). The author concludes that this stability was in defiance of market forces and could only be institutionally based.

[9] A. B. Atkinson: *Is rising income inequality inevitable? A critique of the transatlantic consensus*, WIDER Annual Lectures 3 (Helsinki, United Nations University, World Institute for Development Economics Research, 1999).

[10] D. Dollar and A. Kraay: *Growth is good for the poor*, mimeo. (Washington, DC, World Bank, 2000).

[11] A. Sen: *Reform options and poverty alleviation in India*, mimeo. (New Delhi, 1996), later published in G. K. Chadha and A. N. Sharma (eds): *Growth, employment and poverty: Change and continuity in rural India* (Delhi, Indian Society of Labour Economics, 1997).

[12] Sen discounts the possibility of improved targeting of anti-poverty programmes on the poor as a means of explaining poverty reduction. Clearly, much is known about the relative effectiveness of different types of anti-poverty programmes (see M. Lipton: *Successes in anti-poverty*, Geneva, ILO, 1997). However, there is little evidence that governments are consistently selecting and carrying out more effective programmes (see F. Stewart and W. van der Geest: *Adjustment and social funds: Political panacea or effective policy reduction*, ILO Employment Paper, No. 2, Geneva, 1995). If statistics are to be believed, rural wages were rising faster in the 1980s in India than in Indonesia, despite a much larger share of wage labour in agriculture in India around 1990 (39 per cent) than in Indonesia (12 per cent) and faster per capita income growth in the latter. Probably in Indonesia wage labour, being so much more rare than in India, was used only for relatively high value-added activities and the returns to these increased only slowly, while low value-added activities were phased out. Poverty fell faster than wages rose. Another route from government expenditure to rural poverty alleviation, probably through the provision of better irrigation and other infrastructure, would need to be posited.

[13] M. Ravallion and G. Datt: *Growth and poverty in rural India*, Background paper for the 1995 *World Development Report*, WPS No. 1405 (Washington, DC, World Bank, 1995).

[14] H. Binswanger and J. Quizon: "What can agriculture do for the poorest rural groups?", in I. Adelman and S. Lane (eds): *The balance between industry and agriculture in economic development* (New York, St. Martin's Press, in association with the International Economic Association, 1989).

[15] The "law of one price", that is, commodity arbitrage, may not always occur. Nonetheless, even partial import liberalization is likely to have an effect on domestic prices. See J. Levinsohn: "Testing the imports-as-market-discipline hypothesis", in *Journal of International Economics*, Vol. 35, No. 1–2, Aug. 1993.

[16] Blejer and Khan were able to show that one-quarter of any increase in credit to the private sector was likely to be translated into investment, that foreseeable public investment in line with past trends was associated with increased private investment and that public infrastructure investment was favourable and other public investment not. Nonetheless, the main stimulus to private investment was output growth. See A. Blejer and M. Khan: *Government policy and private investment in developing countries*, Staff Papers (Washington, DC, IMF, June 1984).

[17] Fischer has explained capital accumulation and TFP growth in terms of such policy-related variables as inflation, the budget deficit and the black market foreign exchange premium. While his results generally argue for fiscal prudence, it is clear that substantial budget deficits have often been compatible with growth over long periods. See S. Fischer: "The role of macroeconomic factors in growth", in *Journal of Monetary Economics*, Vol. 32, No. 3, Dec. 1993.

[18] R. Barro: "Government spending in a simple model of endogenous growth", in *Journal of Political Economy*, Vol. 98, No. 5, 1990.

[19] S. Knack: *Governance and employment*, ILO Employment and Training Working Paper, No. 45 (Geneva, 1999).

[20] Mancur Olson (IRIS Center Working Paper No. 137, Maryland, Center for Institutional Reform and the Informal Sector, University of Maryland, 1994) has gone further, arguing that much of the poverty in the developing world is the result of institutions set up by politically well-connected individuals and groups (who tend to be well off) to further their own interests.

[21] See S. Knack and P. Keefer: "Institutions and economic performance: Cross-country tests using alternative institutional measures", in *Economics and Politics*, Vol. 7, Nov. 1995.

[22] This has five elements: the rule of law; quality of the bureaucracy; corruption in government; risk of expropriation of private property; and risk of governments' repudiating contracts.

[23] R. Summers and A. Heston: "The Penn World Tables (Mark V): An extended set of international comparisons, 1950–88", in *Quarterly Journal of Economics*, Vol. 106, No. 2, May 1991.

[24] See, for example, T. Persson and G. Tabellini: "Is inequality harmful for growth?", in *American Economic Review*, Vol. 84, No. 3, June 1994.

[25] See K. Schmidt-Hebbel and L. Serven: *Income inequality and aggregate savings*, World Bank Policy Research Working Paper, No. 1561 (Washington, DC, Jan. 1996).

[26] See A. Alesina and D. Rodrik: "Distributive policies and economic growth", in *Quarterly Journal of Economics*, Vol. CIX, Issue 2, May 1994.

[27] H. Li and H. Zou: "Income inequality is not harmful for growth: Theory and evidence", in *Review of Development Economics*, Vol. 2, No. 3, 1998.

[28] K. Deininger and P. Olinto: *Asset distribution, inequality and growth* (Washington, DC, World Bank, 2000).

[29] Higher levels of education for all are usually associated with faster growth and hence poverty alleviation. While widespread education may spring from a relatively equal income distribution, it need by no means lend itself to greater income equality.

[30] P. Keefer and S. Knack: *Polarization, politics and property rights*, World Bank Working Paper No. 2418 (Washington, DC, 2000).

[31] This is not to say that the operation of institutions can prevent increasing wage inequality if market forces are strongly causing it. But it appears that institutions can significantly mitigate the increase in inequality. It may not be a coincidence that some of the poor in the United States are working full time and that many workers are actively discouraged from joining a union. The relative level of the minimum wage has also fallen over time.

[32] Problems for smaller enterprises also arise frequently because technology transfer from richer to poorer countries occurs largely through multinationals, without any public intervention or guidance.

[33] The usual example given is that of Hoover's transfer of production from a French to a Scottish site in 1993 (see P. Raines: *Labour standards and industrial restructuring in Western Europe*, Employment and Training Paper No. 7, Geneva, ILO, 1998). This appears to have spurred movement towards greater union negotiating flexibility at the plant level.

[34] See K. Bronferbrenner: *The effects of plant closing, or the threat of plant closing, on the right of workers to organize*, Report to the Labor Secretariat of the North American Commission for Labor Cooperation, 1996 (cited in B. Campbell et al.: *Labour market effects under CUFTA/NAFTA*, Employment and Training Paper No. 29, Geneva, ILO, 1999).

[35] Some fear that wages will be pushed down to the level of, for example, Mexico, Poland or China. But the bottom line is that democratic processes in richer countries will set a limit to the amount of acceptable wage dispersion. Furthermore, high levels of education, infrastructure and public administration in richer countries will continue to give them a comparative advantage for many years to come.

[36] The group of experts on social aspects of problems of European economic integration, chaired by Bertil Ohlin in late 1955 and early 1956, considered broadly that different approaches to social policy and social protection in Europe would not distort trade flows. This was essentially because such differences would not change average wage levels, that is, the workers were both the beneficiaries and the financiers of social policy. But the group recognized that the distribution of income between groups of workers (for example, men and women) could be affected by different social policies, which might distort trade flows. (See ILO: *Social aspects of European integration*, Geneva, 1956.)

[37] The contribution of country inequality in income distribution to global inequality is apparently only around 12 per cent. See the article in the *Financial Times*, 25 February 2000, by M. Lundberg and B. Milanovic: "The truth about global inequality", based on the latter's paper for the World Bank: B. Milanovic: *True world income distribution, 1988 and 1993*, World Bank Policy Research Working Paper No. 2244 (Washington, DC, 1999).

[38] It is worth recalling that the ILO's Declaration of Philadelphia (1944) gave the ILO the responsibility to "examine and consider all international economic policies and measures" in the light of the fundamental objective of attaining the conditions in which all human beings have the right to pursue their material well-being and spiritual development. The ILO has also pledged to cooperate fully with international bodies entrusted with the task of expanding production, avoiding economic fluctuations, and promoting development and a steady volume of world trade.

[39] The 88th Session of the International Labour Conference in 2000 called on the ILO to make proposals for revising the Recommendation, stressing the role of social dialogue in training.

# INDEX

Note: Page numbers in *italic* refer to tables and figures. Subscript numbers appended to a page number indicate the endnote number.

*see also* exchange rates
borrowing, risks of 118–19
Botswana 40
Brazil 42, *42*, 43
budget deficits 62, 97, $102_{30}$, $128_{17}$
Bulgaria *30*, 31, 32
  economic data 91, *92*, 93, *94*, *95*
Burkina Faso 41
business investment 88, 89–90, 110

Cambodia $21_{33}$
Canada 74, *75*, *78*, *84*
  demand conditions *78*, 79, 80
  employment growth *25*, *45*, 46, 82, 87, *88*
  investment *81*
  labour productivity 81, *82*, 88
  and NAFTA 117–18
  unemployment rate *24*, 46
capital accumulation $128_{17}$
capital flows 68, 72, $100_9$, 105
  liberalization of 115, 118–19
capital markets
  access to 123
  depth of 17, 18
Caribbean *see* Latin American and the Caribbean
caste system, and discrimination 54
casual workers 15, 34, 50
Central and Eastern Europe xiii, $58_4$, 62, 91
  discrimination 52, 54
  employment rates 29–33
  labour costs $58_6$
  labour market development 18, 57
  macroeconomic problems 91, 94, 117
  privatization 94–7
  structural adjustment 90–100
  trade and GDP 91, *92*
  trade unions 51
  unemployment rates 1, 7, 29–33, *30*
  wage rates 31
  *see also* Central Europe; individual countries
Central Europe $21_{33}$, 29, 73, 91
  employment growth rate *25*, *25*
  unemployment rate 7, *24*

CEPRs *see* country employment policy reviews
child labour 10, $20_{24}$, $59_{24}$, 123, 126
  worst forms of 3, 126–7
childcare 7, 29, 85, 125, 126
Chile 41, *42*, 70
China $20_{21}$, $21_{33}$, 35–6
  economic policies 35, 65, 116–17
  employment rates 25, *25*, *37*
  income growth 106, 107
  labour force 36, *37*, 53
  rural poverty 7, 37, 117, 119
  unemployment levels 7, 23, *24*, 117
  urban poverty $58_{10}$, 110
CIS (Commonwealth of Independent States) $21_{33}$, 99–100
  employment rates 25, *25*, 29
  unemployment rates 7, *24*
  *see also* Russian Federation; Ukraine
civil liberties 12, $20_{25}$, 111
civil society 12
collective bargaining 3, 56, $59_{24}$, $101–2_{26}$, 115, 124, 126
  and flexibility 124
  OECD countries *75*
  *see also* trade unions
collective enterprise, China 36, *37*
Colombia 10, 41, *42*, 43, 70, 71
Comecon (Council for Mutual Economic Assistance) 29, 91
Commonwealth of Independent States *see* CIS
communism 7, 29–30, 90–1
competition 2, 3, 62, 63
  in financial markets 66
  micro-level 13, 61
  and privatization 94
  trade 91, 105
  transition economies 18, 99
comprehensive employment strategy missions (ILO) 10
Congo, Democratic Republic of $58_{16}$
consumer expenditure 89
contracts 86, 111, 124
  temporary, fixed and short-term 31, 40, 50, 61
corporate governance 99